Building Python Real-Time Applications with Storm

Learn to process massive real-time data streams using Storm and Python—no Java required!

Kartik Bhatnagar

Barry Hart

[PACKT]
PUBLISHING

open source*
community experience distilled

BIRMINGHAM - MUMBAI

Building Python Real-Time Applications with Storm

First published: November 2015

Production reference: 1261115

Published by Packt Publishing Ltd.
Livery Place
35 Livery Street
Birmingham B3 2PB, UK.

ISBN 978-1-78439-285-7

www.packtpub.com

Credits

Authors
Kartik Bhatnagar

Barry Hart

Reviewers
Oscar Campos

Pavan Narayanan

Commissioning Editor
Usha Iyer

Acquisition Editor
Larissa Pinto

Content Development Editor
Anish Sukumaran

Technical Editor
Tanmayee Patil

Copy Editor
Vikrant Phadke

Project Coordinator
Izzat Contractor

Proofreader
Safis Editing

Indexer
Rekha Nair

Production Coordinator
Aparna Bhagat

Cover Work
Aparna Bhagat

About the Authors

Kartik Bhatnagar loves nature and likes to visit picturesque places. He is a technical architect in the big data analytics unit of Infosys. He is passionate about new technologies. He is leading the development work of Apache Storm and MarkLogic NoSQL for a leading bank. Kartik has a total 10 years of experience in software development for Fortune 500 companies in many countries. His expertise also includes the full Amazon Web Services (AWS) stack and modern open source libraries. He is active on the StackOverflow platform and is always eager to help young developers with new technologies. Kartik has also worked as a reviewer of a book called *Elasticsearch Blueprints*, *Packt Publishing*. In the future, he wants to work on predictive analytics.

Barry Hart began using Storm in 2012 at AirSage. He quickly saw the potential of Storm while suffering from the limitations of the basic storm.py that it provides. In response, he developed Petrel, the first open source library for developing Storm applications in pure Python. He also contributed some bug fixes to the core Storm project.

When it comes to development, Barry has worked on a little of everything: Windows printer drivers, logistics planning frameworks, OLAP engines for the retail industry, database engines, and big data workflows.

Barry is currently an architect and senior Python/C++ developer at Pindrop Security, helping fight phone fraud in banking, insurance, investment, and other industries.

I want to thank my wonderful wife, Beth, for all her love and support. I would also like to thank my two little boys, who keep me young and make every day special.

About the Reviewers

Oscar Campos has been working with Python since early 2007. He is the author of the famous Anaconda Python IDE package for Sublime Text 3, available as free software at `http://github.com/DamnWidget/anaconda`.

He currently works as a senior software engineer on EXADS, programming high-concurrency backend system applications in Golang.

Oscar has also reviewed *PySide GUI Application Development*, *Packt Publishing*.

I want to thank my wife, Lydia, for all her support in every aspect of my life—without you, nothing could be possible.

Pavan Narayanan is a blogger at DataScience Hacks (`https://datasciencehacks.wordpress.com`), experienced in developing mathematical programming and data analytics solutions. He has utilized Apache Storm for developing real-time analytics prototype and his interests are exploring problem solving techniques, from industrial mathematics to machine learning. He can be reached at `pavan.narayanan@gmail.com`.

Pavan has also reviewed *Apache Mahout Essentials*, *Learning Apache Mahout Classification*, and *Mastering Machine Learning with R*, all by Packt Publishing.

I would like to thank my family and God almighty for all the strength and endurance, and the folks at Packt Publishing for the opportunity to work on this book.

www.PacktPub.com

Support files, eBooks, discount offers, and more

For support files and downloads related to your book, please visit www.PacktPub.com.

Did you know that Packt offers eBook versions of every book published, with PDF and ePub files available? You can upgrade to the eBook version at www.PacktPub.com and as a print book customer, you are entitled to a discount on the eBook copy. Get in touch with us at service@packtpub.com for more details.

At www.PacktPub.com, you can also read a collection of free technical articles, sign up for a range of free newsletters and receive exclusive discounts and offers on Packt books and eBooks.

https://www2.packtpub.com/books/subscription/packtlib

Do you need instant solutions to your IT questions? PacktLib is Packt's online digital book library. Here, you can search, access, and read Packt's entire library of books.

Why subscribe?

- Fully searchable across every book published by Packt
- Copy and paste, print, and bookmark content
- On demand and accessible via a web browser

Free access for Packt account holders

If you have an account with Packt at www.PacktPub.com, you can use this to access PacktLib today and view 9 entirely free books. Simply use your login credentials for immediate access.

Table of Contents

Preface

Apache Storm is a powerful framework for creating complex workflows that ingest and process huge amounts of data. With its generic concepts of spouts and bolts, along with simple deployment and monitoring tools, it allows developers to focus on the specifics of their workflow without reinventing the wheel.

However, Storm is written in Java. While it supports other programming languages besides Java, the tools are incomplete and there is little documentation and few examples.

One of the authors of this book created Petrel, the first framework that supports the creation of Storm topologies in 100 percent Python. He has firsthand experience with the struggles of building a Python Storm topology on the Java tool set. This book closes this gap, providing a resource to help Python developers of all experience levels in building their own applications using Storm.

What this book covers

Chapter 1, *Getting Acquainted with Storm*, provides detailed information about Storm's use cases, different installation modes, and configuration in Storm.

Chapter 2, *The Storm Anatomy*, tells you about Storm-specific terminologies, processes, fault tolerance in Storm, tuning parallelism in Storm, and guaranteed tuple processing, with detailed explanations about each of these.

Chapter 3, *Introducing Petrel*, introduces a framework called Petrel for building Storm topologies in Python. This chapter walks through the installation of Petrel and includes a simple example.

Chapter 4, Example Topology – Twitter, provides an in-depth example of a topology that computes statistics on Twitter data in real time. The example introduces the use of tick tuples, which are useful for topologies that need to compute statistics or do other things on a schedule. In this chapter, you also see how topologies can access configuration data.

Chapter 5, Persistence Using Redis and MongoDB, updates the sample Twitter topology for the use of Redis, a popular key-value store. It shows you how to simplify the complex Python calculation logic with built-in Redis operations. The chapter concludes with an example of storing Twitter data in MongoDB, a popular NoSQL database, and using its aggregation capabilities to generate reports.

Chapter 6, Petrel in Practice, teaches practical skills that will make developers more productive using Storm. You learn how to use Petrel to create automated tests for your spout and bolt components that run outside of Storm. You also see how to use a graphical debugger to debug a topology running inside Storm.

Appendix, Managing Storm Using Supervisord, is a practical demonstration of monitoring and control of Storm using a supervisor over the cluster.

What you need for this book

You will need a computer with Python 2.7, Java 7 JDK, and Apache Storm 0.9.3. Ubuntu is recommended but not required.

Who this book is for

This book is for beginners as well as advanced Python developers who want to use Storm to process big data in real time. While familiarity with the Java runtime environment is helpful for installing and configuring Storm, all the code examples in this book are in Python.

Conventions

In this book, you will find a number of styles of text that distinguish between different kinds of information. Here are some examples of these styles, and an explanation of their meaning.

Code words in text, database table names, folder names, filenames, file extensions, pathnames, dummy URLs, user input, and Twitter handles are shown as follows: "Storm configurations can be done using `storm.yaml`, which is present in the `conf` folder".

A block of code is set as follows:

```
import nltk.corpus

from petrel import storm
from petrel.emitter import BasicBolt

class SplitSentenceBolt(BasicBolt):
    def __init__(self):
        super(SplitSentenceBolt, self).__init__(script=__file__)
        self.stop = set(nltk.corpus.stopwords.words('english'))
        self.stop.update(['http', 'https', 'rt'])
```

When we wish to draw your attention to a particular part of a code block, the relevant lines or items are set in bold:

```
import logging
from collections import defaultdict

from petrel import storm
from petrel.emitter import BasicBolt
```

Any command-line input or output is written as follows:

```
tail -f petrel24748_totalrankings.log
```

New terms and **important words** are shown in bold. Words that you see on the screen, in menus or dialog boxes for example, appear in the text like this: "Finally, click on **Create your Twitter application**".

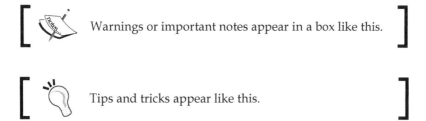

> Warnings or important notes appear in a box like this.

> Tips and tricks appear like this.

Reader feedback

Feedback from our readers is always welcome. Let us know what you think about this book—what you liked or may have disliked. Reader feedback is important for us to develop titles that you really get the most out of.

To send us general feedback, simply send an e-mail to feedback@packtpub.com, and mention the book title via the subject of your message.

If there is a topic that you have expertise in and you are interested in either writing or contributing to a book, see our author guide on www.packtpub.com/authors.

Customer support

Now that you are the proud owner of a Packt book, we have a number of things to help you to get the most from your purchase.

Downloading the example code

You can download the example code files for all Packt books you have purchased from your account at http://www.packtpub.com. If you purchased this book elsewhere, you can visit http://www.packtpub.com/support and register to have the files e-mailed directly to you.

Errata

Although we have taken every care to ensure the accuracy of our content, mistakes do happen. If you find a mistake in one of our books—maybe a mistake in the text or the code—we would be grateful if you would report this to us. By doing so, you can save other readers from frustration and help us improve subsequent versions of this book. If you find any errata, please report them by visiting http://www.packtpub. com/submit-errata, selecting your book, clicking on the **errata submission form** link, and entering the details of your errata. Once your errata are verified, your submission will be accepted and the errata will be uploaded on our website, or added to any list of existing errata, under the Errata section of that title. Any existing errata can be viewed by selecting your title from http://www.packtpub.com/support.

Piracy

Piracy of copyright material on the Internet is an ongoing problem across all media. At Packt, we take the protection of our copyright and licenses very seriously. If you come across any illegal copies of our works, in any form, on the Internet, please provide us with the location address or website name immediately so that we can pursue a remedy.

Please contact us at copyright@packtpub.com with a link to the suspected pirated material.

We appreciate your help in protecting our authors, and our ability to bring you valuable content.

Questions

You can contact us at questions@packtpub.com if you are having a problem with any aspect of the book, and we will do our best to address it.

1
Getting Acquainted with Storm

In this chapter, you will get acquainted with the following topics:

- An overview of Storm
- The "before Storm" era and key features of Storm
- Storm cluster modes
- Storm installation
- Starting various daemons
- Playing with Storm configurations

Over the complete course of the chapter, you will learn why Storm is creating a buzz in the industry and why it is relevant in present-day scenarios. What is this real-time computation? We will also explain the different types of Storm's cluster modes, the installation, and the approach to configuration.

Overview of Storm

Storm is a distributed, fault-tolerant, and highly scalable platform for processing streaming data in a real-time manner. It became an Apache top-level project in September 2014, and was previously an Apache Incubator project since September 2013.

Real-time processing on a massive scale has become a requirement of businesses. Apache Storm provides the capability to process data (a.k.a tuples or stream) as and when it arrives in a real-time manner with distributed computing options. The ability to add more machines to the Storm cluster makes Storm scalable. Then, the third most important thing that comes with storm is fault tolerance. If the storm program (also known as topology) is equipped with reliable spout, it can reprocess the failed tuples lost due to machine failure and also give fault tolerance. It is based on XOR magic, which will be explained in *Chapter 2*, *The Storm Anatomy*.

Storm was originally created by Nathan Marz and his team at BackType. The project was made open source after it was acquired by Twitter. Interestingly, Storm received a tag as Real Time Hadoop.

Storm is best suited for many real-time use cases. A few of its interesting use cases are explained here:

- **ETL pipeline**: ETL stands for **Extraction**, **Transformation**, and **Load**. It is a very common use case of Storm. Data can be extracted or read from any source. Here, the data can be complex XML, a JDBC result set row, or simply a few key-value records. Data (also known as tuples in Storm) can be enriched on the fly with more information, transformed into the required storage format, and stored in a NoSQL/RDBMS data store. All of these things can be achieved at a very high throughput in a real-time manner with simple storm programs. Using the Storm ETL pipeline, you can ingest into a big data warehouse at high speed.

- **Trending topic analysis**: Twitter uses such use cases to know the trending topics within a given time frame or at present. There are numerous use cases, and finding the top trends in a real-time manner is required. Storm can fit well in such use cases. You can also perform running aggregation of values with the help of any database.

- **Regulatory check engine**: Real-time event data can pass through a business-specific regulatory algorithm, which can perform a compliance check in a real-time manner. Banks use these for trade data checks in real time.

Storm can ideally fit into any use case where there is a need to process data in a fast and reliable manner, at a rate of more than 10,000 messages processing per second, as soon as data arrives. Actually, 10,000+ is a small number. Twitter is able to process millions of tweets per second on a large cluster. It depends on how well the Storm topology is written, how well it is tuned, and the cluster size.

Storm program (a.k.a topologies) are designed to run 24x7 and will not stop until someone stops them explicitly.

Storm is written using both Clojure as well as Java. Clojure is a Lisp, functional programming language that runs on JVM and is best for concurrency and parallel programming. Storm leverages the mature Java library, which was built over the last 10 years. All of these can be found inside the storm/lib folder.

Before the Storm era

Before Storm became popular, real-time or near-real-time processing problems were solved using intermediate brokers and with the help of message queues. Listener or worker processes run using the Python or Java languages. For parallel processing, code was dependent on the threading model supplied using the programming language itself. Many times, the old style of working did not utilize CPU and memory very well. In some cases, mainframes were used as well, but they also became outdated over time. Distributed computing was not so easy. There were either many intermediate outputs or hops in this old style of working. There was no way to perform a fail replay automatically. Storm addressed all of these pain areas very well. It is one of the best real-time computation frameworks available for use.

Key features of Storm

Here are Storm's key features; they address the aforementioned problems:

- **Simple to program**: It's easy to learn the Storm framework. You can write code in the programming language of your choice and can also use the existing libraries of that programming language. There is no compromise.

- **Storm already supports most programming languages**: However, even if something is not supported, it can be done by supplying code and configuration using the JSON protocol defined in the Storm **Data Specification Language (DSL)**.

- **Horizontal scalability or distributed computing is possible**: Computation can be multiplied by adding more machines to the Storm cluster without stopping running programs, also known as topologies.

- **Fault tolerant**: Storm manages worker and machine-level failure. Heartbeats of each process are tracked to manage different types of failure, such as task failure on one machine or an entire machine's failure.

- **Guaranteed message processing**: There is a provision of performing auto and explicit ACK within storm processes on messages (tuples). If ACK is not received, storm can do a reply of a message.

- **Free, open source, and lots of open source community support**: Being an Apache project, Storm has free distribution and modifying rights without any worry about the legal aspect. Storm gets a lot of attention from the open source community and is attracting a large number of good developers to contribute to the code.

Storm cluster modes

The Storm cluster can be set up in four flavors based on the requirement. If you want to set up a large cluster, go for distributed installation. If you want to learn Storm, then go for a single machine installation. If you want to connect to an existing Storm cluster, use client mode. Finally, if you want to perform development on an IDE, simply unzip the storm TAR and point to all dependencies of the storm library. At the initial learning phase, a single-machine storm installation is actually what you need.

Developer mode

A developer can download storm from the distribution site, unzip it somewhere in $HOME, and simply submit the Storm topology as local mode. Once the topology is successfully tested locally, it can be submitted to run over the cluster.

Single-machine Storm cluster

This flavor is best for students and medium-scale computation. Here, everything runs on a single machine, including **Zookeeper**, **Nimbus**, and **Supervisor**. Storm/bin is used to run all commands. Also, no extra Storm client is required. You can do everything from the same machine. This case is well demonstrated in the following figure:

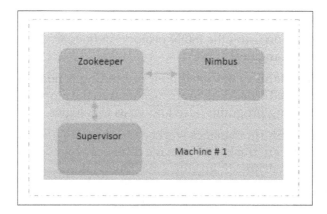

Multimachine Storm cluster

This option is required when you have a large-scale computation requirement. It is a horizontal scaling option. The following figure explains this case in detail. In this figure, we have five physical machines, and to increase fault tolerance in the systems, we are running Zookeeper on two machines. As shown in the diagram, **Machine 1** and **Machine 2** are a group of Zookeeper machines; one of them is the leader at any point of time, and when it dies, the other becomes the leader. **Nimbus** is a lightweight process, so it can run on either machine, 1 or 2. We also have **Machine 3**, **Machine 4**, and **Machine 5** dedicated for performing actual processing. Each one of these machines (3, 4, and 5) requires a supervisor daemon to run over there. Machines 3, 4, and 5 should know where the Nimbus/Zookeeper daemon is running and that entry should be present in their `storm.yaml`.

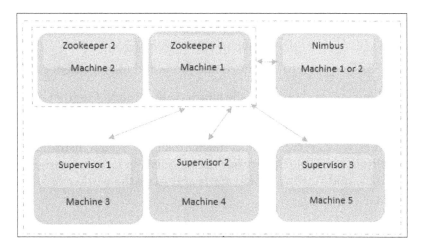

So, each physical machine (3, 4, and 5) runs one supervisor daemon, and each machine's `storm.yaml` points to the IP address of the machine where Nimbus is running (this can be 1 or 2). All Supervisor machines must add the Zookeeper IP addresses (1 and 2) to `storm.yaml`. The Storm UI daemon should run on the Nimbus machine (this can be 1 or 2).

The Storm client

The Storm client is required only when you have a Storm cluster of multiple machines. To start the client, unzip the Storm distribution and add the Nimbus IP address to the `storm.yaml` file. The Storm client can be used to submit Storm topologies and check the status of running topologies from command-line options. Storm versions older than 0.9 should put the `yaml` file inside `$STORM_HOME/.storm/storm.yaml` (not required for newer versions).

The `jps` command is a very useful Unix command for seeing
the Java process ID of Zookeeper, Nimbus, and Supervisor. The
`kill -9 <pid>` option can stop a running process. The `jps`
command will work only when `JAVA_HOME` is set in the `PATH`
environment variable.

Prerequisites for a Storm installation

Installing Java and Python is easy. Let's assume our Linux machine is ready with
Java and Python:

- A Linux machine (Storm version 0.9 and later can also run on
  Windows machines)
- Java 6 (set export `PATH=$PATH:$JAVA_HOME/bin`)
- Python 2.6 (required to run Storm daemons and management commands)

We will be making lots of changes in the storm configuration file (that is, `storm.
yaml`), which is actually present under `$STORM_HOME/config`. First, we start the
Zookeeper process, which carries out coordination between Nimbus and the
Supervisors. Then, we start the Nimbus master daemon, which distributes code
in the Storm cluster. Next, the Supervisor daemon listens for work assigned
(by Nimbus) to the node it runs on and starts and stops the worker processes
as necessary.

ZeroMQ/JZMQ and Netty are inter-JVM communication libraries that permit two
machines or two JVMs to send and receive process data (tuples) between each other.
JZMQ is a Java binding of ZeroMQ. The latest versions of Storm (0.9+) have now
been moved to Netty. If you download an old version of Storm, installing ZeroMQ
and JZMQ is required. In this book, we will be considering only the latest versions
of Storm, so you don't really require ZeroMQ/JZMQ.

Zookeeper installation

Zookeeper is a coordinator for the Storm cluster. The interaction between Nimbus
and worker nodes is done through Zookeeper. The installation of Zookeeper is well
explained on the official website at `http://zookeeper.apache.org/doc/trunk/
zookeeperStarted.html#sc_InstallingSingleMode`.

The setup can be downloaded from:

`https://archive.apache.org/dist/zookeeper/zookeeper-3.3.5/zookeeper-3.3.5.tar.gz`. After downloading, edit the `zoo.cfg` file.

The following are the Zookeeper commands that are used:

- Starting the `zookeeper` process:

  `../zookeeper/bin/./zkServer.sh start`

- Checking the running status of the `zookeeper` service:

  `../zookeeper/bin/./zkServer.sh status`

- Stopping the `zookeeper` service:

  `../zookeeper/bin/./zkServer.sh stop`

Alternatively, use `jps` to find `<pid>` and then use `kill -9 <pid>` to kill the processes.

Storm installation

Storm can be installed in either of these two ways:

1. Fetch a Storm release from this location using Git:

   ◦ `https://github.com/nathanmarz/storm.git`

2. Download directly from the following link: `https://storm.apache.org/downloads.html`

Storm configurations can be done using `storm.yaml`, which is present in the `conf` folder.

The following are the configurations for a single-machine Storm cluster installation.

Port # `2181` is the default port of Zookeeper. To add more than one `zookeeper`, keep entry – separated:

```
storm.zookeeper.servers:
    - "localhost"


# you must change 2181 to another value if zookeeper running on another
port.
storm.zookeeper.port: 2181
# In single machine mode nimbus run locally so we are keeping it
localhost.
```

```
# In distributed mode change localhost to machine name where nimbus
daemon is running.
```

`nimbus.host: "localhost"`

```
# Here storm will generate logs of workers, nimbus and supervisor.
```

`storm.local.dir: "/var/stormtmp"`

`java.library.path: "/usr/local/lib"`

```
# Allocating 4 ports for workers. More numbers can also be added.
```

`supervisor.slots.ports:`

- 6700

- 6701

- 6702

- 6703

```
# Memory is allocated to each worker. In below case we are allocating 768
mb per worker.worker.childopts: "-Xmx768m"
```

```
# Memory to nimbus daemon- Here we are giving 512 mb to nimbus.
```

`nimbus.childopts: "-Xmx512m"`

```
# Memory to supervisor daemon- Here we are giving 256 mb to supervisor.
```

> Notice `supervisor.childopts: "-Xmx256m"`. In this setting, we reserved four supervisor ports, which means that a maximum of four worker processes can run on this machine.

`storm.local.dir`: This directory location should be cleaned if there is a problem with starting Nimbus and Supervisor. In the case of running a topology on the local IDE on a Windows machine, `C:\Users\<User-Name>\AppData\Local\Temp` should be cleaned.

Enabling native (Netty only) dependency

Netty enables inter JVM communication and it is very simple to use

Netty configuration

You don't really need to install anything extra for Netty. This is because it's a pure Java-based communication library. All new versions of Storm support Netty.

Add the following lines to your `storm.yaml` file. Configure and adjust the values to best suit your use case:

```
storm.messaging.transport: "backtype.storm.messaging.netty.Context"

storm.messaging.netty.server_worker_threads: 1

storm.messaging.netty.client_worker_threads: 1

storm.messaging.netty.buffer_size: 5242880

storm.messaging.netty.max_retries: 100

storm.messaging.netty.max_wait_ms: 1000

storm.messaging.netty.min_wait_ms: 100
```

Starting daemons

Storm daemons are the processes that are needed to pre-run before you submit your program to the cluster. When you run a topology program on a local IDE, these daemons auto-start on predefined ports, but over the cluster, they must run at all times:

1. Start the master daemon, `nimbus`. Go to the `bin` directory of the Storm installation and execute the following command (assuming that `zookeeper` is running):

    ```
    ./storm nimbus
    ```

    ```
    Alternatively, to run in the background, use the same command
    with nohup, like this:
    ```

    ```
    Run in background
    ```

    ```
    nohup ./storm nimbus &
    ```

2. Now we have to start the `supervisor` daemon. Go to the `bin` directory of the Storm installation and execute this command:

    ```
    ./storm supervisor
    ```

    To run in the background, use the following command:

    ```
    nohup ./storm  supervisor &
    ```

 If Nimbus or the Supervisors restart, the running topologies are unaffected as both are stateless.

3. Let's start the `storm` UI. The Storm UI is an optional process. It helps us to see the Storm statistics of a running topology. You can see how many executors and workers are assigned to a particular topology. The command needed to run the storm UI is as follows:

```
./storm ui
```

Alternatively, to run in the background, use this line with `nohup`:

```
nohup ./storm ui &
```

To access the Storm UI, visit `http://localhost:8080`.

4. We will now start `storm logviewer`. Storm UI is another optional process for seeing the log from the browser. You can also see the `storm` log using the command-line option in the `$STORM_HOME/logs` folder. To start logviewer, use this command:

```
./storm logviewer
```

To run in the background, use the following line with `nohup`:

```
nohup ./storm logviewer &
```

 To access Storm's log, visit `http://localhost:8000log viewer` daemon should run on each machine. Another way to access the log of `<machine name>` for worker port `6700` is given here:

```
<Machine name>:8000/log?file=worker-6700.log
```

5. DRPC daemon: DRPC is another optional service. **DRPC** stands for **Distributed Remote Procedure Call**. You will require the DRPC daemon if you want to supply to the storm topology an argument externally through the DRPC client. Note that an argument can be supplied only once, and the DRPC client can wait for long until storm topology does the processing and the return. DRPC is not a popular option to use in projects, as firstly, it is blocking to the client, and secondly, you can supply only one argument at a time. DRPC is not supported by Python and Petrel.

Summarizing, the steps for starting processes are as follows:

1. First, all the Zookeeper daemons.
2. Nimbus daemons.
3. Supervisor daemon on one or more machine.

4. The UI daemon where Nimbus is running (optional).

5. The Logviewer daemon (optional).

6. Submitting the topology.

You can restart the `nimbus` daemon anytime without any impact on existing processes or topologies. You can restart the supervisor daemon and can also add more supervisor machines to the Storm cluster anytime.

To submit `jar` to the Storm cluster, go to the `bin` directory of the Storm installation and execute the following command:

```
./storm jar <path-to-topology-jar> <class-with-the-main> <arg1> … <argN>
```

Playing with optional configurations

All the previous settings are required to start the cluster, but there are many other settings that are optional and can be tuned based on the topology's requirement. A prefix can help find the nature of a configuration. The complete list of default `yaml` configuration is available at `https://github.com/apache/storm/blob/master/conf/defaults.yaml`.

Configurations can be identified by how the prefix starts. For example, all UI configurations start with `ui*`.

Nature of the configuration	Prefix to look into
General	`storm.*`
Nimbus	`nimbus.*`
UI	`ui.*`
Log viewer	`logviewer.*`
DRPC	`drpc.*`
Supervisor	`supervisor.*`
Topology	`topology.*`

All of these optional configurations can be added to STORM_HOME/conf/storm.yaml for any change other than the default values. All settings that start with topology.* can either be set programmatically from the topology or from storm.yaml. All other settings can be set only from the storm.yaml file. For example, the following table shows three different ways to play with these parameters. However, all of these three do the same thing:

/conf/storm.yaml	Topology builder	Custom yaml
Changing storm.yaml (impacts all the topologies of the cluster)	Changing the topology builder while writing code (impacts only the current topology)	Supplying topology.yaml as a command-line option (impacts only the current topology)
topology.workers: 1	conf. setNumberOfWorker(1); This is supplied through Python code	Create topology.yaml with the entry made into it similar to storm.yaml, and supply it when running the topology Python: petrel submit --config topology. yaml

Any configuration change in storm.yaml will affect all running topologies, but when using the conf.setXXX option in code, different topologies can overwrite that option, what is best suited for each of them.

Summary

Here comes the conclusion of the first chapter. This chapter gave an overview of how applications were developed before Storm came into existence. A brief knowledge of what real-time computations are and how Storm, as a programming framework, is becoming so popular was also acquired as we went through the chapter and approached the conclusion. This chapter taught you to perform Storm configurations. It also gave you details about the daemons of Storm, Storm clusters, and their step up. In the next chapter, we will be exploring the details of Storm's anatomy.

The Storm Anatomy

2

This chapter gives a detailed view of the internal structure and processes of the Storm technology. We will cover the following topics in this chapter:

- Storm processes
- Storm-topology-specific terminologies
- Interprocess communication
- Fault tolerance in Storm
- Guaranteed tuple processing
- Parallelism in Storm — scaling a distributed computation

As we advance through the chapter, you will understand Storm's processes and their role in detail. In this chapter, various Storm-specific terminologies will be explained. You will learn how Storm achieves fault tolerance for different types of failure. We will see what guaranteed message processing is and, most importantly, how to configure parallelism in Storm to achieve fast and reliable processing.

Storm processes

We will start with Nimbus first, which is actually the entry-point daemon in Storm. Just to compare with Hadoop, Nimbus is actually the job tracker of Storm. Nimbus's job is to distribute code to all supervisor daemons of a cluster. So, when topology code is submitted, it actually reaches all physical machines in the cluster. Nimbus also monitors failure of supervisors. If a supervisor continues to fail, then Nimbus reassigns those workers' jobs to other workers of a different physical machine. The current version of Storm allows only one instance of the Nimbus daemon to run. Nimbus is also responsible for assigning tasks to supervisor nodes. If you lose Nimbus, the workers will still continue to compute. Supervisors will continue to restart workers as and when they die. Without Nimbus, a worker's task won't be reassigned to another machine worker within the cluster.

There is no alternative Storm process that will take over if Nimbus dies, and no process will even try to restart it. There is nothing to worry about, however, since it can be restarted anytime. In a production environment, alerts can also be set when Nimbus dies. In future, we may see highly available Nimbus.

Supervisor

A supervisor manages all the workers of the respective machine. Distributed computation in Storm is possible due to the supervisor daemon, as there is one supervisor per machine in your cluster. The supervisor daemon listens for the work assigned by Nimbus to the machine that it runs, and distributes it among workers. Due to any runtime exception, workers can die anytime, and the supervisor restarts them when there is no heartbeat from dead workers. Each worker process executes a part of a topology. Similar to the Hadoop ecosystem, supervisor is a task tracker of Storm. It tracks the tasks of workers of the same machine. The maximum number of possible workers depends on the number of ports defined in `storm.yaml`.

Zookeeper

In addition to its own components, Storm relies on a Zookeeper cluster (one or more Zookeeper servers) to perform the coordination job between Nimbus and the supervisors. Apart from using Zookeeper for coordination purposes, Nimbus and the supervisors also store all their states in Zookeeper, and Zookeeper stores them on a local disk where it is running. Having more than one Zookeeper daemon increases the reliability of the system, because if one daemon goes down, another becomes the leader.

The Storm UI

Storm is also equipped with a web-based user interface. It should be started on a machine that also runs Nimbus. The Storm UI provides a report of the entire cluster, such as the sum of all active supervisor machines, the total number of workers available, allotted to each topology and how many remaining, and topology-level diagnostics such as tuples stats (how many tuples were emitted, and the ACK between spout to bolt or bolt to bolt). The Storm UI also shows the total number of workers, which is actually sum of all workers available of all supervisors' machines.

The following screenshot shows a sample screen of the Storm UI:

Topology stats

Window		Emitted	Transferred	Complete latency (ms)
10m 0s		1797920	1796900	22375.223
3h 0m 0s		1797920	1796900	22375.223
1d 0h 0m 0s		1797920	1796900	22375.223
All time		1797920	1796900	22375.223

Spouts (All time)

Id		Executors	Tasks	Emitted	Transferred	Complete latency
kafkaLogReadingSpout		10	10	794350	794300	22375.223

Bolts (All time)

Id		Executors	Tasks	Emitted	Transferred	Capacity (last 10m)	Execute latency (ms)
__acker		15	15	11620	11630	0.010	0.019
aggregatorBolt		200	200	106920	106160	1.500	438.744
kafkaMsgBolt		5	5	791440	791420	0.608	1.523
persistanceBolt		5	5	20	0	0.103	1.267
persistancePrepreationBolt		5	5	93360	93340	0.624	0.486

Following is the explanation of Storm UI:

- **Topology stats**: Under **Topology stats**, you can click and see the stats of the last 10 minutes, 3 hours, or all time.

- **Spouts (All time)**: This displays the number of executors and tasks assigned for this spout, along with the stats of emitted tuples and other latency stats.

- **Bolts (All time)**: This displays a list of all bolts, along with the assigned executors/tasks. When you are doing performance tuning, keep the **Capacity** column close to 1. In the preceding example for **aggregatorBolt**, it is 1.500, so instead of 200 executors/tasks, we can use 300. The **Capacity** column helps us decide the right degree of parallelism. The idea is very simple; if the **Capacity** column reads more than 1, try increasing the executors and tasks in the same ratio. If the value of executors/tasks is high and the **Capacity** column is close to zero, try reducing the number of executors/tasks. You can do this until you get the best configuration.

Storm-topology-specific terminologies

A topology is a logical separation of programming work into many small-scale processing units called spout and bolt, which is similar to MapReduce in Hadoop. A topology can be written in many languages, including Java, Python, and lot more supported languages. In visual depictions, a topology is shown as a graph of connecting spouts and bolts. Spouts and bolts execute tasks across the cluster. Storm has two modes of operation, called local mode and distributed mode:

- In local mode, all processes of Storm and workers run within your code development environment. This is good for testing and development of topologies.

- In distributed mode, Storm operates as a cluster of machines. When you submit topology code to the Nimbus, Nimbus takes care of distributing the code and allocating workers to run your topology based on your configuration.

In the following figure, we have purple bolts; these receive a tuple or records from the spout above them. A tuple supports most of the data types available in the programming language in which the topology code is being written. It flows as an independent unit from a spout to a bolt or a bolt to another bolt. An unbounded flow of tuples is called a stream. In a single tuple, you can have many key-value pairs to pass together.

The next figure illustrates streams in more detail. A spout is connected to a source of tuples and generates continuous tuples for the topology as a stream. What you emit from the spout as a key-value pair can be received by the bolt using the same key.

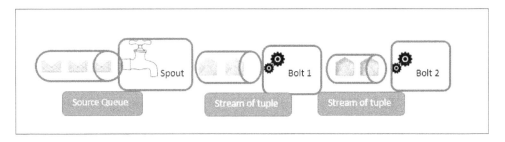

The worker process, executor, and task

Storm distinguishes between the following three main entities, which are used to actually run a topology in a Storm cluster:

- Worker
- Executor
- Task

Let's say we have decided to keep two workers, one spout executor, three **Bolt1** executors, and two **Bolt2** executors. Assume that the ratio of the number of executors and tasks is the same. The total sum of executors is six for spout and bolt. Out of six executors, some will run within the scope of worker 1, and some will be in control of worker 2; this decision is taken by the supervisor. This is explained in the following figure:

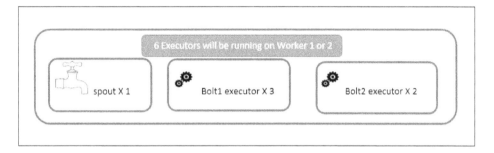

The next figure explains the position of the workers and executors within the scope of the supervisor that is running on a machine:

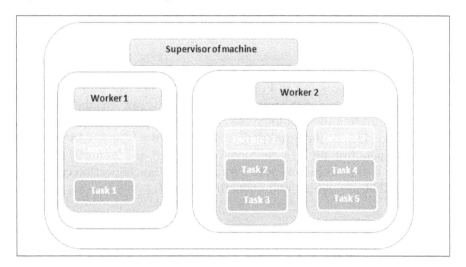

The number of executors and tasks is set while building the topology code. In the preceding figure, we have two workers (1 and 2), run and managed by the supervisor of that machine. Assume that **Executor 1** is running one task, because the ratio of executors to tasks is the same (for example, 10 executors means 10 tasks, which makes the ratio 1:1). But **Executor 2** is running two tasks sequentially, so the ratio of tasks to executors is 2:1 (for example, 10 executors means 20 tasks, which makes the ratio 2:1). Having more tasks never means higher processing speed, but this is true for more executors, as tasks run sequentially.

Worker processes

A single worker process executes a portion of a topology and runs on its own JVM. Workers are allocated during topology submission. A worker process is linked to a specific topology and can run one or more executors for one or more spouts or bolts of that topology. A running topology consists of many such workers running on many machines within a Storm cluster.

Executors

An executor is a thread run within the scope of a worker's JVM. An executor may run one or more tasks for a spout or bolt sequentially.

An executor always runs on one thread for all its tasks, which means that tasks run serially on an executor. The number of executors can be changed after the topology has been started without shutdown, using the `rebalance` command:

```
storm rebalance <topology name> -n <number of workers> -e
<spout>=<number of executors> -e <bolt1 name>=<number of
executors> -e <bolt2 name>=<number of executors>
```

Tasks

A task performs data processing and runs within its parent executor's thread of execution. The default value of the number of tasks is the same as the number of executors. While building the topology, we can keep a higher number of tasks as well. It can help to increase the number of executors in the future, which keeps the scope of scaling open. Initially, we can have 10 executors and 20 tasks, so the ratio is 2:1. This means two tasks per executor. A future rebalancing action can make 20 executors and 20 tasks, which will make the ratio 1:1.

Interprocess communication

The following figure illustrates communication between the Storm submitter (client), the Nimbus thrift server, Zookeeper, supervisors, workers of supervisors, executors, and tasks. Each worker process runs as a separate JVM.

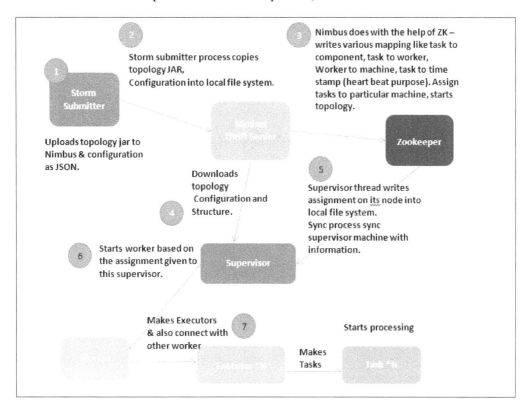

A physical view of a Storm cluster

The next figure explains the physical position of each process. There can be only one Nimbus. However, more than one Zookeeper is there to support failover, and per machine, there is one supervisor.

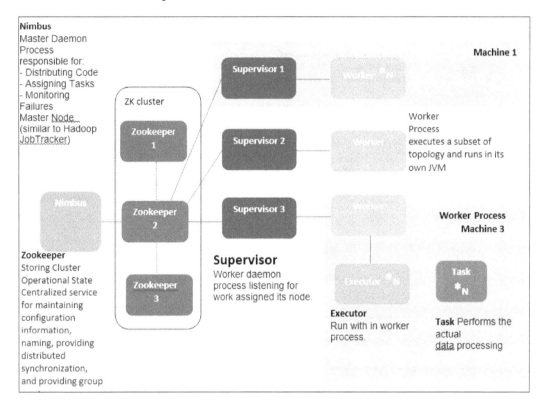

Stream grouping

A stream grouping controls the flow of tuples between from spout to bolt or bolt to bolt. In Storm, we have four types of groupings. Shuffle and field grouping are most commonly used:

- **Shuffle grouping**: Tuple flow between two random tasks in this grouping
- **Field grouping**: A tuple with a particular field key is always delivered to the same task of the downstream bolt
- **All grouping**: Sends the same tuple to all tasks of the downstream bolt
- **Global grouping**: Tuples from all tasks reach one task

The subsequent figure gives a diagrammatic explanation of all the four types of groupings:

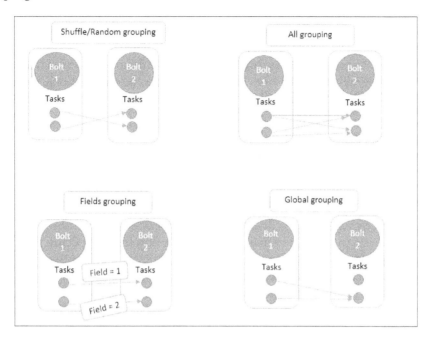

Fault tolerance in Storm

Supervisor runs a synchronization thread to get assignment information (what part of topology I am supposed to run) from Zookeeper and write to the local disk. This local filesystem information helps keep the worker up to date:

- **Case 1**: This is the ideal case for most of the times. When the cluster works normally, the worker's heartbeat goes back to the supervisors and Nimbus via Zookeeper.

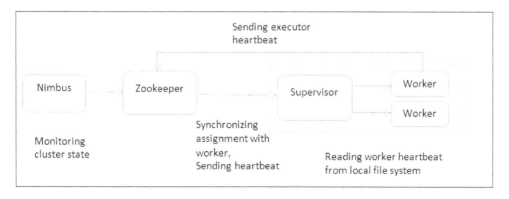

- **Case 2**: If a supervisor dies, processing still continues, but the assignment is never synchronized. Nimbus will reassign the work to another supervisor of a different machine. Those workers will be running, but will not receive any new tuples. Do set an alert to restart the supervisor or use a Unix tool that can restart the supervisor.

- **Case 3**: If Nimbus dies, the topologies will continue to function normally. Processing will still continue, but topology life cycle operations and reassigning to another machine will not be possible.

- **Case 4**: If a worker dies (as the heartbeat stops arriving), the supervisor will try to restart the worker process and processing will continue. If a worker dies repeatedly, Nimbus will reassign the work to other nodes in the cluster.

Guaranteed tuple processing in Storm

As Storm is already equipped to deal with various process-level failures, another important feature is the ability to deal with failure of tuples that occurs when a worker dies. This is just to give an idea of bitwise XOR: the XOR of two sets of the same bits is 0. This is called XOR magic, and it can help us know whether the delivery of a tuple to the next bolt is successful or not. Storm uses 64 bits to track tuples. Every tuple gets a 64-bit tuple ID. This 64-bit ID, along with the task ID, is kept at ACKer.

In the next figure, ACKing and a replay case is explained:

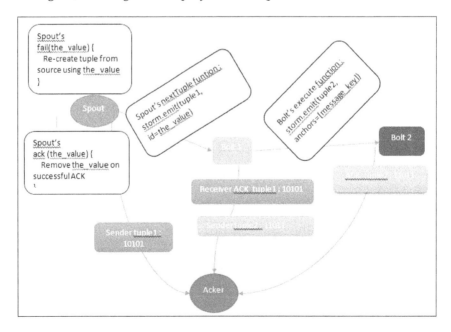

XOR magic in acking

A spout tuple is not fully processed until all the tuples in the linked tuple tree are completed. If the tuple tree is not completed within a configured timeout (the default value is `topology.message.timeout.secs: 30`), the spout tuple is replayed.

In the preceding diagram, the first acker gets `10101` (for simplicity of explanation, we are keeping 5 bits) for tuple 1 from the spout. Once **Bolt 1** receives the same tuple, it also ACK to acker. From both sources, acker gets `10101`. This means `10101 XOR 10101 = 0`. Tuple 1 is successfully received by **Bolt 1**. The same process repeats between bolts 1 and 2. At last, **Bolt 2** sends ack to acker, and the tuple tree is completed. This creates a signal to call the spout's `success` function. Any failure in tuple processing can trigger the spout's `fail` function call, which gives an indication to send the tuple back for processing again.

Storm's acker tracks the completion of the tuple tree by performing XOR between the sender's tuple and the receiver's tuple. Each time a tuple is sent, its value is XORed into the checksum maintained by acker, and each time a tuple is acked, its value is XORed in again at acker.

If all tuples have been successfully acked, the checksum will be zero. Ackers are system-level executors.

In the spout, we have a choice of two emit functions.

- `emit([tuple])`: This is a simple emit
- `storm.emit([tuple], id=the_value)`: This creates a reliable spout, but only if you can re-emit a tuple using `the_value`

In the Spout, we also have two ACK functions:

- `fail(the_value)`: This function is called when a timeout occurs or the tuple fails
- `ack(the_value)`: This function is called when the last bolt of the topology ACK the tuple tree

This ID field should be a random and unique value to replay from the spout's `fail` function. Using this ID, we can re-emit it from the `fail` function. If successful, the jn `success` function will call and it can remove successful tuples from the global list or recreate from the source.

You will be able to recreate the same tuple if you have a reliable spout in the topology. To create a reliable spout, emit a unique message ID (`the_value`) from the spout's next tuple function along with the tuple:

```
storm.emit([tuple], id=the_value)
```

Whether a tuple is not ACKed within a configured period of time, or the programming code fails a tuple due to some error condition, both are valid cases of replay.

When the `fail` function is called, the code can read from the source of the spout using the same message ID, and when the `success` function is called, an action such as removing a message from the queue can be taken.

The message ID is an application-specific key that can help you recreate a tuple and emit it back from the spout. An example of a message ID can be a queue message ID, or a primary key of a table. A tuple is considered failed if a timeout occurs or due to any other reason.

Storm has a fault tolerance mechanism that guarantees at-least-once processing for all tuples emitted only from a reliable spout.

Once you have a reliable spout in place, you can make the bolt do the linking between the input and output tuples, which creates a tuple tree. Once a tuple tree is established, acker knows any failure in the linked tree, and the original message ID is used to create the entire tuple tree again.

In the bolt, there are two functions:

- `emit([tuple])`: There is no tuple tree linking. We can't track which original message ID was used.

- `storm.emit([tuple], anchors=[message_key])`: With linking in place, the original tuple can now be replayed.

The following figure explains how tuple B is generated from tuple A:

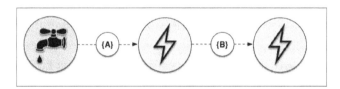

The next figure illustrates the bolt performing **ACK**:

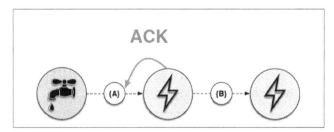

The following figure illustrates the failure condition, where the signal reaches the spout upon failure:

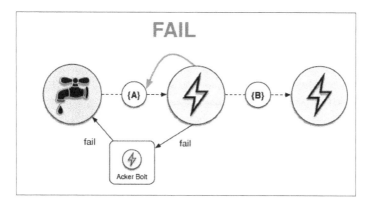

A successful **ACK** is demonstrated as follows:

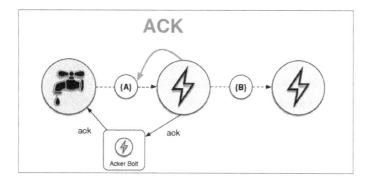

The following figure illustrates a condition of a big tuple tree without a bolt, and there is no failure:

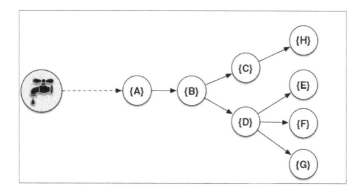

The next figure demonstrates an example of failure in a tuple tree—in the middle of the tuple tree:

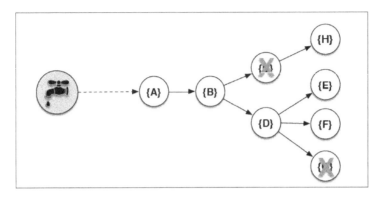

Tuning parallelism in Storm – scaling a distributed computation

To explain parallelism of Storm, we will configure three parameters:

- The number of workers
- The number of executors
- The number of tasks

The following figure gives a diagrammatic explanation of an example where we have a topology with just one spout and one bolt. In this case, we will set different values for the numbers of workers, executors, and tasks at the spout and bolt levels, and see how parallelism works in each case:

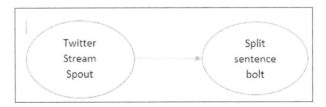

```
// assume we have two workers in total for topology.
topology.workers: 2
  // just one executor of spout.
builder.setSpout("spout-sentence", TwitterStreamSpout(),1)
```

```
// two executors of bolt.
builder.setBolt("bolt-split", SplitSentenceBolt(),2)
  // four tasks for bolts.
.setNumTasks(4)
.shuffleGrouping("spout-sentence");
```

For this configuration, we will have two workers, which will run in separate JVMs (worker 1 and worker 2).

For the spout, there is one executor, and the default number of tasks is one, which makes the ratio 1:1 (one task per executor).

For the bolt, there are two executors and four tasks, which makes it 4/2 = two tasks per executor. These two executors run under worker 2, with each having two tasks, while the executor of worker 1 gets only one task.

This can be illustrated nicely using the following figure:

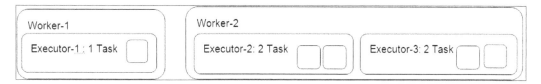

Let's change the configuration in the bolt to two executors and two tasks:

```
builder.setBolt("bolt-split", SplitSentenceBolt(),2)
  // 2 tasks for bolts.
.setNumTasks(2)
.shuffleGrouping("spout-sentence");
```

This can be illustrated well here:

The number of workers is two again. As the bolt has two executors and two tasks, that makes it 2/2, or one task per executor. Now you can see that both executors get one task each. In terms of performance, both cases are exactly the same, as the tasks run sequentially within the executor thread. More executors means a higher degree of parallelism, and more workers means using resources such as CPU and RAM more effectively. Memory allocation is done at the worker level using the `worker.childopts` setting. We should also monitor the maximum amount of memory a particular worker process is holding. This plays an important role in deciding the total number of workers. It can be seen using the `ps -ef` option. Always keep the tasks and executors in the same ratio, and derive the correct value for the number of executors using the capacity column of the Storm UI. As an important note, we should keep the shorter duration transaction in the bolt and try to tune it via splitting code into more bolts or reducing the batch size tuple. The batch size is the number of records received by the bolt in a single tuple delivery. Also, don't block the `nextTuple` method of the spout due to the longer holding transaction.

Summary

As this chapter approaches its end, you must have got a brief idea about the Nimbus, supervisor, UI, and Zookeeper processes. This chapter also taught you how to tune parallelism in Storm by playing with the number of workers, executors, and tasks. You became familiar with the important problem of distributing computation, that is, failures and overcoming failures by different kinds of fault tolerance available in the system. And most importantly, you learned how to write a "reliable" spout to achieve guaranteed message processing and linking in bolts.

The next chapter will give you information about how to build a simple topology using a Python library called Petrel. Petrel addresses some limitations of Storm's built-in Python support, providing simpler and more streamlined development.

3
Introducing Petrel

As discussed in *Chapter 1*, *Getting Acquainted with Storm*, Storm is a platform for processing large amounts of data in real time. Storm applications are often written in Java, but Storm supports other languages as well, including Python. While the concepts are similar across languages, the details vary by language. In this chapter, we'll get our first hands-on experience using Storm with Python. First, you'll learn about a Python library called Petrel, which is necessary for creating topologies in Python. Next, we'll set up our Python/Storm development environment. Then, we'll take a close look at a working Storm topology written in Python. Finally, we'll run the topology and you will learn some key techniques to ease the process of developing and debugging topologies. After you complete this chapter, you'll have a good high-level understanding of developing basic Storm topologies. In this chapter, we will cover these topics:

- What is Petrel?
- Installing Petrel
- Creating your first topology
- Running the topology
- Productivity tips with Petrel

What is Petrel?

All Python topologies in this book rely on an open source Python library called Petrel. If you have prior experience with Storm, you may recall that there is a GitHub project called `storm-starter` that includes examples of using Storm with various languages (you can find the latest version of `storm-starter` at `https://github.com/apache/storm/tree/master/examples/storm-starter`). The `storm-starter` project includes a module called `storm.py`, which allows you to implement Storm topologies in Python. Given the availability of `storm.py`, is it really necessary to use another library? While it is certainly possible to build topologies using `storm.py`, it lacks some important features. To work around those gaps, a developer must use languages and tools that won't be familiar to most Python developers. If you are already familiar with these tools and do not mind juggling multiple technology stacks as you work with Storm, you may be happy with `storm.py`. But most developers who are new to Storm find the `storm.py` approach to be overly complex, even overwhelming. Let's discuss the weaknesses of `storm.py` in more detail.

Building a topology

In order to run a topology, Storm needs a description of spouts, bolts, and streams within it. This description is encoded in a format called **Thrift**. The `storm.py` module does not support the creation of this description; the developer must create it using another programming language (typically Java or Clojure).

Packaging a topology

A topology is submitted to Storm in the form of a Java `.jar` file (similar to Python `.egg` or `.tar.gz` files). In addition to the topology description, a Python topology `.jar` must also include the Python code for the topology. Creating a JAR file typically involves using Java development tools such as Ant or Maven.

Logging events and errors

It is much easier to debug and monitor a topology if it includes logging messages to allow tracking of the data that flows through it. If things go wrong in a Python topology and the code crashes, it's invaluable to see what the error was and where it occurred. The `storm.py` module provides no help in these areas. If a component crashes, it simply exits without capturing any information. In my experience, this is the most frustrating aspect of working with `storm.py`.

Managing third-party dependencies

Real-world Python applications often use third-party libraries. If a cluster needs to run multiple topologies, each topology may have different, even conflicting versions of these libraries. Python virtual environments are a great tool for managing this. However, `storm.py` does not help you create, activate, or install third-party libraries in a Python virtual environment. Petrel addresses all of these limitations of Storm's built-in Python support, providing a simpler, more streamlined development experience. Petrel's key features include the following:

- A Python API for building a topology

- Packaging a topology for submission to Storm

- Logging events and errors

- On worker nodes, setting up a topology-specific Python runtime environment using `setup.sh`

In this chapter, we'll talk about the first three points. We'll see an example of the fourth in *Chapter 4*, *Example Topology – Twitter*.

Installing Petrel

Let's set up our Python development environment. We assume here that you have already followed the instructions in *Chapter 1*, *Getting Acquainted with Storm*, to install Storm 0.9.3:

1. First, we need to install `virtualenv`, a tool for managing Python libraries. On Ubuntu, simply run this command:

   ```
   sudo apt-get install python-virtualenv
   ```

2. Next, we create a Python virtual environment. This provides a way to install Python libraries without requiring root access to the machine and without interfering with the system's Python packages:

   ```
   virtualenv petrel
   ```

   You will see something like the following output:

   ```
   New python executable in petrel/bin/python
   Installing distribute.........................................
   ............................................................
   ............................................................
   .............done
   ```

3. Next, run this command to activate the virtual environment. Your shell prompt will change to include the `virtualenv` name, indicating that the virtual environment is active:

```
source petrel/bin/activate

(petrel)barry@Dell660s:~$
```

 You'll need to run this command again—each time you open a new terminal.

4. Finally, install Petrel:

```
easy_install petrel==0.9.3.0.3
```

 The first three digits of the Petrel version number must match the version of Storm that you're using. If you're using a version of Storm with no corresponding Petrel release, you can install Petrel from source. Check out `https://github.com/AirSage/Petrel#installing-petrel-from-source` for instructions.

 Downloading the example code

You can download the example code files for all Packt books you have purchased from your account at http://www.packtpub.com. If you purchased this book elsewhere, you can visit http://www.packtpub.com/supportand register to have the files e-mailed directly to you

Creating your first topology

Now, we'll create a Storm topology that breaks sentences into words and then counts the number of occurrences of each word. Implementing this topology in Storm requires the following components:

- Sentence spout (`randomsentence.py`): A topology always begins with a spout; that's how data gets into Storm. The sentence spout will emit an infinite stream of sentences.

- Splitter bolt (`splitsentence.py`): This receives sentences and splits them into words.

- Word count bolt (`wordcount.py`): This receives words and counts the occurrences. For each word processed, output the word along with the number of occurrences.

The following figure shows how data flows through the topology:

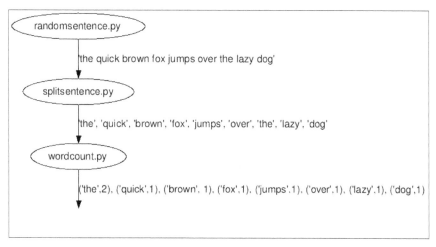

Word count topology

Now that we've seen the basic data flow, let's implement the topology and see how it works.

Sentence spout

In this section, we implement a spout that generates random sentences. Enter this code in a file called randomsentence.py:

```
import time
import random

from petrel import storm
from petrel.emitter import Spout

class RandomSentenceSpout(Spout):
    def __init__(self):
        super(RandomSentenceSpout, self).__init__(script=__file__)

    @classmethod
    def declareOutputFields(cls):
        return ['sentence']

    sentences = [
        "the cow jumped over the moon",
        "an apple a day keeps the doctor away",
    ]
```

```
    def nextTuple(self):
        time.sleep(0.25)
        sentence = self.sentences[
            random.randint(0, len(self.sentences) - 1)]
        storm.emit([sentence])


def run():
    RandomSentenceSpout().run()
```

The spout inherits from Petrel's `Spout` class.

Petrel requires every spout and bolt class to implement __init__() and pass its filename to the (script=__file__) base class. The `script` parameter tells Petrel which Python script to run while launching an instance of the component.

The `declareOutputFields()` function tells Storm about the structure of the tuples emitted by this spout. Each tuple consists of a single field named `sentence`.

Storm calls `nextTuple()` each time it is ready for more data from the spout. In a real-world spout, you might be reading from an external data source, such as Kafka or Twitter. This spout is just an example, so it generates its own data. It simply makes a random choice between one of two sentences.

You may have noticed that the spout sleeps for 0.25 seconds on every call to `nextTuple()`. Why is this so? It's not technically necessary, but it slows things down and makes the output easier to read when the topology runs in local mode.

What does the `run()` function do? It's a bit of *glue* code required by Petrel. When a spout or bolt script is loaded into Storm, Petrel calls the `run()` function to create the component and begins processing messages. If your spout or bolt needs to do additional initialization, this is a good place for it to do so.

Splitter bolt

This section provides the splitter bolt, which consumes sentences from the spout and splits them into words. Enter this code in a file called `splitsentence.py`:

```
from petrel import storm
from petrel.emitter import BasicBolt

class SplitSentenceBolt(BasicBolt):
    def __init__(self):
        super(SplitSentenceBolt, self).__init__(script=__file__)
```

```
    def declareOutputFields(self):
        return ['word']

    def process(self, tup):
        words = tup.values[0].split("")
        for word in words:
          storm.emit([word])

def run():
    SplitSentenceBolt().run()
```

SplitSentenceBolt inherits from the BasicBolt Petrel class. This class is used for most simple bolts. You may recall that Storm has a feature for ensuring that every message is processed, "replaying" previous tuples if they were not processed to completion. BasicBolt simplifies working with this feature. It does so by automatically acknowledging to Storm as each tuple is processed. The more flexible Bolt class allows the programmer to directly acknowledge tuples, but is it beyond the scope of this book.

The split sentence bolt has a run function, similar to the spout.

The process() function receives sentences from the spout and splits them into words. Each word is emitted as an individual tuple.

Word Counting Bolt

This section implements the word count bolt, which consumes words from the spout and counts them. Enter the following code in the wordcount.py file:

```
from collections import defaultdict

from petrel import storm
from petrel.emitter import BasicBolt

class WordCountBolt(BasicBolt):
    def __init__(self):
        super(WordCountBolt, self).__init__(script=__file__)
        self._count = defaultdict(int)

    @classmethod
    def declareOutputFields(cls):
        return ['word', 'count']

    def process(self, tup):
        word = tup.values[0]
```

```
        self._count[word] += 1
        storm.emit([word, self._count[word]])

def run():
    WordCountBolt().run()
```

The word count bolt has a new wrinkle; unlike the sentence bolt, it needs to store information from one tuple to the next—the word count. The __init__() function sets up a _count field to handle this.

The word count bolt uses Python's handy defaultdict class, which simplifies counting things by automatically providing a 0 entry when we access a nonexistent key.

Defining a topology

The previous sections provided the spout and bolts for the word count topology. Now, we need to tell Storm how the components combine to form a topology. In Petrel, this is done with a create.py script. This script provides the following information:

- Spouts and bolts that make up the topology
- For each bolt, where its input data comes from
- How tuples are partitioned among the instances of the bolt

Here is the create.py script:

```
from randomsentence import RandomSentenceSpout
from splitsentence import SplitSentenceBolt
from wordcount import WordCountBolt

def create(builder):
    builder.setSpout("spout", RandomSentenceSpout(), 1)
    builder.setBolt(
        "split", SplitSentenceBolt(), 1).shuffleGrouping("spout")
    builder.setBolt(
        "count", WordCountBolt(), 1).fieldsGrouping(
        "split", ["word"])
```

It is vital that the word count bolt uses Storm's fieldsGrouping behavior (as described in the *Stream grouping* section of *Chapter 2, The Storm Anatomy*).This setting for a bolt lets you group the tuples in your data stream on one or more fields. For the word count topology, fieldsGrouping ensures that all instances of a word will be counted by the same Storm worker process.

When the topology is deployed on a cluster, there will probably be many separate running instances of the word count bolt. If we didn't configure `fieldsGrouping` on the `"word"` field, then we might get the following results by processing the sentence, "the cow jumped over the moon":

```
Word count instance 1: { "the": 1, "cow": 1, "jumped": 1 }
Word count instance 2: { "over": 1, "the": 1, "moon": 1 }
```

There are two entries for `"the"`, and because of this, the count is wrong! We want something like this instead:

```
Word count instance 1: { "the": 2, "cow": 1, "jumped": 1 }
Word count instance 2: { "over": 1, "moon": 1 }
```

Running the topology

Just a few more details and we'll be ready to run the topology:

1. Create a `topology.yaml` file. This is a configuration file for Storm. A complete explanation of this file is beyond the scope of this book, but you can see the entire set of available options at `https://github.com/apache/storm/blob/master/conf/defaults.yaml`:

    ```
    nimbus.host: "localhost"
    topology.workers: 1
    ```

2. Create an empty `manifest.txt` file. You can use an editor to do this or simply run `touch manifest.txt`. This is a Petrel-specific file that tells Petrel what additional files (if any) should be included in the `.jar` file that it submits to Storm. In *Chapter 4, Example Topology – Twitter* we'll see an example that really uses this file.

3. Before running the topology, let's review the list of files we've created. Make sure you have created these files correctly:

    -   `randomsentence.py`
    -   `splitsentence.py`
    -   `wordcount.py`
    -   `create.py`
    -   `topology.yaml`
    -   `manifest.txt`

4. Run the topology with the following command:

```
petrel submit --config topology.yaml --logdir `pwd`
```

Congratulations! You have created and run your first topology!

Petrel runs the `create.py` script to discover the structure of the topology, and then uses that information plus the `manifest.txt` file to build a `topology.jar` file and submit it to Storm. Next, Storm unpacks the `topology.jar` file and prepares the workers. With Petrel, this requires creating a Python virtual environment and installing Petrel from the Internet. In about 30 seconds, the topology will be up and running in Storm.

You'll see an endless stream of output, sprinkled with messages similar to the following:

```
25057 [Thread-20] INFO  backtype.storm.daemon.task - Emitting:
split default ["the"]

25058 [Thread-20] INFO  backtype.storm.daemon.task - Emitting:
split default ["moon"]

25059 [Thread-22] INFO  backtype.storm.daemon.task - Emitting:
count default ["cow",3]

25059 [Thread-9-count] INFO  backtype.storm.daemon.executor -
Processing received message source: split:3, stream: default, id:
{}, ["over"]

25059 [Thread-9-count] INFO  backtype.storm.daemon.executor -
Processing received message source: split:3, stream: default, id:
{}, ["the"]

25059 [Thread-9-count] INFO  backtype.storm.daemon.executor -
Processing received message source: split:3, stream: default, id:
{}, ["moon"]

25060 [Thread-22] INFO  backtype.storm.daemon.task - Emitting:
count default ["jumped",3]

25060 [Thread-22] INFO  backtype.storm.daemon.task - Emitting:
count default ["over",3]

25060 [Thread-22] INFO  backtype.storm.daemon.task - Emitting:
count default ["the",9]

25060 [Thread-22] INFO  backtype.storm.daemon.task - Emitting:
count default ["moon",3]
```

5. When you've seen enough, press *Ctrl* + *C* to kill Storm. Sometimes, it doesn't exit cleanly. If it doesn't, typically the following steps will clean things up: press *Ctrl* + *C* a few more times, and press *Ctrl* + *Z* to pause Storm.

6. Type `ps` to get a list of `processes`Look for a Java process and get its process `id`Type `"kill -9 processid"`, replacing `processid` with the ID of the Java process.

Troubleshooting

If the topology doesn't run correctly, review the log files created in the current directory. Errors are often caused by using a version of Storm that does not have a corresponding version of Petrel on the PyPI website (`https://pypi.python.org/pypi/petrel`). At the time of writing this book, two Storm versions are supported:

- 0.9.3
- 0.9.4

If you are using an unsupported version of Storm, you are likely to see an error similar to one of these:

```
  File "/home/barry/.virtualenvs/petrel2/lib/python2.7/site-packages/
petrel-0.9.3.0.3-py2.7.egg/petrel/cmdline.py", line 19, in get_storm_
version
    return m.group(2)
AttributeError: 'NoneType' object has no attribute 'group'


IOError: [Errno 2] No such file or directory: '/home/barry/.virtualenvs/
petrel2/lib/python2.7/site-packages/petrel-0.9.3.0.3-py2.7.egg/petrel/
generated/storm-petrel-0.10.0-SNAPSHOT.jar'
```

Productivity tips with Petrel

We've covered a lot of ground in this chapter. While we don't know every detail of Storm, we've seen how to construct a topology with multiple components and send data between them.

The Python code for the topology is quite short—only about 75 lines in all. This makes a nice example, but really, it's just a little too short. When you start writing your own topologies, things probably won't work perfectly the first time. New code usually has bugs, and may even crash sometimes. To get things working correctly, you'll need to know what's happening in the topology, especially when there are problems. As you work on fixing problems, you'll be running the same topology over and over, and the 30-second startup time for a topology can seem like eternity.

Improving startup performance

Let's address startup performance first. By default, when a Petrel topology starts up, it creates a new Python `virtualenv` and installs Petrel and other dependencies in it. While this behavior is very useful for deploying a topology on a cluster, it is very inefficient during development, when you may be launching the topology dozens of times. To skip the `virtualenv` creation step, simply change the `submit` command to have Petrel reuse the existing Python virtual environment:

```
petrel submit --config topology.yaml --venv self
```

This cuts the startup time from 30 seconds down to about 10 seconds.

Enabling and using logging

Like many languages, Python has a logging framework that provides a way to capture information on what is happening inside a running application. This section describes how to use logging with Storm:

1. In the same directory as that of the word count topology, create a new file, called `logconfig.ini`:

```
[loggers]
keys=root,storm
[handlers]
keys=hand01
[formatters]
keys=form01
[logger_root]
level=INFO
handlers=hand01
[logger_storm]
qualname=storm
level=DEBUG
handlers=hand01
propagate=0
[handler_hand01]
class=FileHandler
level=DEBUG
formatter=form01
args=(os.getenv('PETREL_LOG_PATH') or 'petrel.log', 'a')
[formatter_form01]
format=[%(asctime)s] [%(name)s] [%(levelname)s] %(message)s
datefmt=
class=logging.Formatter
```

What you just saw is a simple log configuration for demonstration purposes. For more information about Python logging, consult the logging module documentation at https://www.python.org/.

2. Update wordcount.py to log its input and output. The newly added lines are highlighted:

```python
import logging
from collections import defaultdict

from petrel import storm
from petrel.emitter import BasicBolt

log = logging.getLogger('wordcount')

class WordCountBolt(BasicBolt):
    def __init__(self):
        super(WordCountBolt, self).__init__(script=__file__)
        self._count = defaultdict(int)

    @classmethod
    def declareOutputFields(cls):
        return ['word', 'count']

    def process(self, tup):
        log.debug('WordCountBolt.process() called with: %s',
                  tup)
        word = tup.values[0]
        self._count[word] += 1
        log.debug('WordCountBolt.process() emitting: %s',
            [word, self._count[word]])
        storm.emit([word, self._count[word]])

def run():
    WordCountBolt().run()
```

3. Now launch the updated topology:

```
petrel submit --config topology.yaml --venv self --logdir `pwd`
```

As the topology runs, a log file for the word count component will be written to the current directory, capturing what's happening. The filename varies from run to run, but it will be something like `petrel22011_wordcount.log`:

```
WordCountBolt.process() called with: <Tuple component='split'
id='5891744987683180633' stream='default' task=3 values=['moon']>

WordCountBolt.process() emitting: ['moon', 2]

WordCountBolt.process() called with: <Tuple component='split' id='-
8615076722768870443' stream='default' task=3 values=['the']>

WordCountBolt.process() emitting: ['the', 7]
```

Automatic logging of fatal errors

If a spout or bolt crashes due to a runtime error, you'll need to know what happened in order to fix it. To help with this, Petrel automatically writes fatal runtime errors to the log:

1. Add a line at the beginning of the word count bolt's `process()` function so that it crashes:

   ```
   def process(self, tup):

       raise ValueError('abc')

       log.debug('WordCountBolt.process() called with: %s', tup)

       word = tup.values[0]

       self._count[word] += 1

       log.debug('WordCountBolt.process() emitting: %s',
           [word, self._count[word]])

       storm.emit([word, self._count[word]])
   ```

2. Run the topology again and examine the word count log file. It'll contain a backtrace for the failure:

   ```
   [2015-02-08 22:28:42,383] [storm] [INFO] Caught exception

   [2015-02-08 22:28:42,383] [storm] [ERROR] Sent failure message
   ("E_BOLTFAILED__wordcount__Dell660s__pid__21794__port__-1__
   taskindex__-1__ValueError") to Storm

   [2015-02-08 22:28:47,385] [storm] [ERROR] Caught exception in
   BasicBolt.run

   Traceback (most recent call last):

      File "/home/barry/dev/Petrel/petrel/petrel/storm.py", line 381,
   in run

          self.process(tup)
   ```

```
   File "/tmp/b46e3137-1956-4abf-80c8-acaa7d3626d1/supervisor/
stormdist/test+topology-1-1423452516/resources/wordcount.py", line
19, in process
   raise ValueError('abc')
```

ValueError: abc

```
[2015-02-08 22:28:47,386] [storm] [ERROR] The error occurred while
processing this tuple: ['an']
```

Worker wordcount exiting normally.

Summary

In this chapter, you learned how Petrel makes it possible to develop Storm topologies in pure Python. We created and ran a simple topology, and you learned how it works. You also learned how to use Petrel's `--venv self` option and Python logging to streamline your development and debugging process.

In the next chapter, we will see some more complex topologies, including a spout that reads from a real-world data source (Twitter), rather than randomly generated data.

4
Example Topology – Twitter

This chapter builds on the material from *Chapter 3, Introducing Petrel*. In this chapter, we'll build a topology that demonstrates a number of new features and techniques. In particular, we'll see how to:

- Implement a spout that reads from Twitter
- Build topology components based on third-party Python libraries
- Compute statistics and rankings over rolling time periods
- Read custom configuration settings from `topology.yaml`
- Use "tick tuples" to execute logic on a schedule

Twitter analysis

Most of you have heard of Twitter, but if you have not, check out how Wikipedia describes Twitter:

> *"an online social networking service that enables users to send and read short 140-character messages called "tweets"."*

In 2013, users posted 400 million messages per day on Twitter. Twitter offers an API that gives developers real-time access to streams of tweets. On it, messages are public by default. The volume of messages, the availability of an API, and the public nature of tweets combine to make Twitter a valuable source of insights on current events, topics of interest, public sentiment, and so on.

Storm was originally developed at BackType to process tweets, and Twitter analysis is still a popular use case of Storm. You can see several examples on the Storm website at `https://storm.apache.org/documentation/Powered-By.html`.

The topology in this chapter demonstrates how to read from Twitter's real-time streaming API, computing a ranking of the most popular words. It's a Python version of the "rolling top words" sample on the Storm website (`https://github.com/apache/storm/blob/master/examples/storm-starter/src/jvm/storm/starter/RollingTopWords.java`), and consists of the following components:

- Twitter stream spout (`twitterstream.py`): This reads tweets from the Twitter sample stream.

- Splitter bolt (`splitsentence.py`): This receives tweets and splits them into words. It is an improved version of the splitter bolt from *Chapter 3, Introducing Petrel*.

- Rolling word count bolt (`rollingcount.py`): This receives words and counts the occurrences. It is similar to the word count bolt from *Chapter 3, Introducing Petrel*, but implements a rolling count (this means that the bolt periodically discards old data, so the word counts only consider recent messages).

- Intermediate rankings bolt (`intermediaterankings.py`): This consumes word counts and periodically emits the *n* most frequently seen words.

- Total rankings bolt (`totalrankings.py`): This is similar to the intermediate rankings bolt. It combines the intermediate rankings to produce an overall set of rankings.

Twitter's Streaming API

Twitter's public API is both powerful and flexible. It has many features for both posting and consuming tweets. Our application needs to receive and process tweets in real time. Twitter's streaming API was designed to solve this problem. In computer science, a *stream* is a sequence of data elements (in this case, tweets) made available over time.

The streaming API is explained in detail at `https://dev.twitter.com/streaming/overview`. To use it, an application first creates a connection to Twitter. The connection remains open indefinitely to receive tweets.

The Streaming API offers several ways to choose which tweets your application receives. Our topology uses the so-called sample stream, which provides a small subset of all tweets arbitrarily chosen by Twitter. The sample stream is intended for demos and testing. Production applications generally use one of the other stream types. For more information about the available streams, refer to `https://dev.twitter.com/streaming/public`.

Creating a Twitter app to use the Streaming API

Before we can use Twitter's Streaming API, Twitter requires us to create an app. This sounds complicated, but it's quite easy to set up; basically, we just fill in a form on the website:

1. If you don't have a Twitter account, create one at `https://twitter.com/`.

2. Once you have an account, log in and go to `https://apps.twitter.com/`. Click on **Create New App**. Fill in the form for creating an application. Leave the **Callback URL** field blank. The default access level is read-only, which means that this application can only read tweets; it can't post or make other changes. Read-only access is fine for this example. Finally, click on **Create your Twitter application**. You will be redirected to your app's page.

3. Click on the **Keys and Access Tokens** tab, then click on **Create my access token**. Twitter will generate an access token consisting of two parts: **Access Token** and **Access Token Secret**. While connecting to Twitter, your application will use this token along with **Consumer Key** and **Consumer Secret**.

The following screenshot shows the **Keys and Access Tokens** tab after generating the access token:

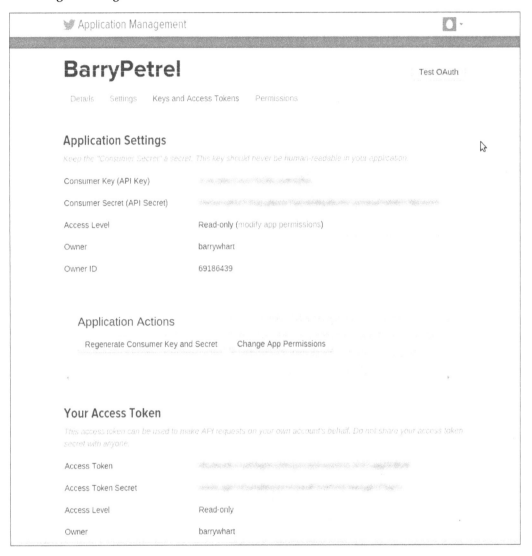

The topology configuration file

Now that we've set up a Twitter account with API access, we're ready to create the topology. First, create topology.yaml. We first saw a basic topology.yaml file in *Chapter 3, Introducing Petrel*. Here, topology.yaml will also hold the connection parameters for Twitter. Enter the following text, replacing the four oauth values with your own Twitter credentials from https://apps.twitter.com/:

```
nimbus.host: "localhost"
topology.workers: 1

oauth.consumer_key: "blahblahblah"
oauth.consumer_secret: "blahblahblah"
oauth.access_token: "blahblahblah"
oauth.access_token_secret: "blahblahblah"
```

The Twitter stream spout

Now, let's look at the Twitter spout. Enter this code in twitterstream.py:

```python
import json
import Queue
import threading

from petrel import storm
from petrel.emitter import Spout

from tweepy.streaming import StreamListener
from tweepy import OAuthHandler, Stream

class QueueListener(StreamListener):
    def __init__(self, queue):
        self.queue = queue

    def on_data(self, data):
        tweet = json.loads(data)
        if 'text' in tweet:
            self.queue.put(tweet['text'])
        return True


class TwitterStreamSpout(Spout):
    def __init__(self):
```

```
            super(TwitterStreamSpout, self).__init__(script=__file__)
            self.queue = Queue.Queue(1000)

    def initialize(self, conf, context):
        self.conf = conf
        thread = threading.Thread(target=self._get_tweets)
        thread.daemon = True
        thread.start()

    @classmethod
    def declareOutputFields(cls):
        return ['sentence']

    def _get_tweets(self):
        auth = OAuthHandler(
            self.conf['oauth.consumer_key'],
            self.conf['oauth.consumer_secret'])
        auth.set_access_token(
            self.conf['oauth.access_token'],
            self.conf['oauth.access_token_secret'])
        stream = Stream(auth, QueueListener(self.queue))
        stream.sample(languages=['en'])

    def nextTuple(self):
        tweet = self.queue.get()
        storm.emit([tweet])
        self.queue.task_done()

def run():
    TwitterStreamSpout().run()
```

How does the spout communicate with Twitter? The Twitter API imposes a number of requirements on API clients:

- Connections must be encrypted using the Secure Sockets Layer (SSL)
- API clients must be authenticated using OAuth, a popular authentication protocol used to interact with secure web services
- Because it involves a long-lived connection, the streaming API involves more than a simple HTTP request

Fortunately, there is a library called **Tweepy** (http://www.tweepy.org/) that implements these requirements in a simple and easy-to-use Python API. Tweepy provides a Stream class to connect to the Streaming API. It is used in _get_tweets().

Creating a Tweepy stream requires the four Twitter connection parameters listed earlier. We could hardcode these directly in our spout, but then we'd have to change the code if the connection parameters change. Instead, we put this information in the topology.yaml configuration file. Our spout reads these settings in the initialize() function. Storm calls this function when a task for this component starts up, passing it information about the environment and configuration. Here, the initialize() function captures the topology configuration in self.conf. This dictionary includes the oauth values.

The following sequence diagram shows how the spout communicates with Twitter, receives tweets, and emits them. You may have noticed that the spout creates a background thread. This thread receives the tweets from Tweepy and passes them to the main spout thread using a Python queue.

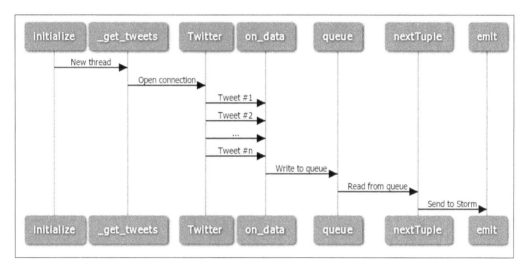

Why does the spout use a thread? Often, threads are used to support concurrent processing. That's not the case here. Rather, there is simply a mismatch between the behavior of Tweepy and the Petrel spout API.

When reading from a Twitter stream, Tweepy blocks execution, calling an application-supplied event handler function for each tweet received.

In Petrel, the nextTuple() function on a spout must return from the function after each tuple.

Running Tweepy in a background thread that writes to a queue provides a simple and elegant solution to these conflicting requirements.

Splitter bolt

The splitter bolt here is similar in structure to the one in *Chapter 3, Introducing Petrel*. This version has two improvements that make it more useful and realistic.

 Ignore words that are so common that they are not interesting or useful in a "top words" list. This includes English words such as "the," as well as word-like terms that appear frequently in Tweets, such as "http," "https," and "rt."

Omit punctuation when splitting a Tweet into words.

A Python library called **Natural Language Toolkit (NLTK)** makes it easy to implement both. NLTK has many other fascinating, powerful language processing features, but those are beyond the scope of this book.

Enter this code in `splitsentence.py`:

```python
import nltk.corpus

from petrel import storm
from petrel.emitter import BasicBolt

class SplitSentenceBolt(BasicBolt):
    def __init__(self):
        super(SplitSentenceBolt, self).__init__(script=__file__)
        self.stop = set(nltk.corpus.stopwords.words('english'))
        self.stop.update(['http', 'https', 'rt'])

    def declareOutputFields(self):
        return ['word']

    def process(self, tup):
        for word in self._get_words(tup.values[0]):
            storm.emit([word])

    def _get_words(self, sentence):
        for w in nltk.word_tokenize(sentence):
            w = w.lower()
            if w.isalpha() and w not in self.stop:
                yield w

def run():
    SplitSentenceBolt().run()
```

Rolling word count bolt

The rolling word count bolt is similar to the word count bolt in *Chapter 3, Introducing Petrel*. The bolt in the earlier chapter simply accumulated the word counts indefinitely. This is not good for analyzing top words on Twitter, where popular topics can change from one moment to the next. Rather, we want counts that reflect the latest information. To do this, the rolling word count bolt stores data in time-based buckets. Then, it periodically discards buckets that exceed 5 minutes in age. Thus, the word counts from this bolt only consider the last 5 minutes of data.

Enter the following code in `rollingcount.py`:

```python
from collections import defaultdict

from petrel import storm
from petrel.emitter import BasicBolt

class SlotBasedCounter(object):
    def __init__(self, numSlots):
        self.numSlots = numSlots
        self.objToCounts = defaultdict(lambda: [0] * numSlots)

    def incrementCount(self, obj, slot):
        self.objToCounts[obj][slot] += 1

    def getCount(self, obj, slot):
        return self.objToCounts[obj][slot]

    def getCounts(self):
        return dict((k, sum(v)) for k, v in
          self.objToCounts.iteritems())

    def wipeSlot(self, slot):
        for obj in self.objToCounts.iterkeys():
            self.objToCounts[obj][slot] = 0

    def shouldBeRemovedFromCounter(self, obj):
        return sum(self.objToCounts[obj]) == 0

    def wipeZeros(self):
        objToBeRemoved = set()
        for obj in self.objToCounts.iterkeys():
            if sum(self.objToCounts[obj]) == 0:
                objToBeRemoved.add(obj)
```

```
        for obj in objToBeRemoved:
            del self.objToCounts[obj]


class SlidingWindowCounter(object):
    def __init__(self, windowLengthInSlots):
        self.windowLengthInSlots = windowLengthInSlots
        self.objCounter = /
            SlotBasedCounter(
                self.windowLengthInSlots)
        self.headSlot = 0
        self.tailSlot = self.slotAfter(self.headSlot)

    def incrementCount(self, obj):
        self.objCounter.incrementCount(obj, self.headSlot)

    def getCountsThenAdvanceWindow(self):
        counts = self.objCounter.getCounts()
        self.objCounter.wipeZeros()
        self.objCounter.wipeSlot(self.tailSlot)
        self.headSlot = self.tailSlot
        self.tailSlot = self.slotAfter(self.tailSlot)
        return counts

    def slotAfter(self, slot):
        return (slot + 1) % self.windowLengthInSlots


class RollingCountBolt(BasicBolt):
    numWindowChunks = 5
    emitFrequencyInSeconds = 60
    windowLengthInSeconds = numWindowChunks * \
        emitFrequencyInSeconds

    def __init__(self):
        super(RollingCountBolt, self).__init__(script=__file__)
        self.counter = SlidingWindowCounter(
            self.windowLengthInSeconds /
                self.emitFrequencyInSeconds

    @classmethod
    def declareOutputFields(cls):
        return ['word', 'count']
```

```
def process(self, tup):
    if tup.is_tick_tuple():
        self.emitCurrentWindowCounts()
    else:
        self.counter.incrementCount(tup.values[0])

def emitCurrentWindowCounts(self):
    counts = self.counter.getCountsThenAdvanceWindow()
    for k, v in counts.iteritems():
        storm.emit([k, v])

def getComponentConfiguration(self):
    return {"topology.tick.tuple.freq.secs":
        self.emitFrequencyInSeconds}


def run():
    RollingCountBolt().run()
```

The SlotBasedCounter stores a list of numSlots (five) count values for each word. Each slot stores emitFrequencyInSeconds (60) seconds of data. Count values more than 5 minutes old are discarded.

How does the bolt know when 60 seconds have elapsed? Storm makes this easy by providing a feature called **tick tuples**. This feature is useful when you need to execute some logic within your bolts as per a schedule. To use this feature, perform the following steps:

- In getComponentConfiguration(), return a dictionary containing a topology.tick.tuple.freq.secs key. The value is the desired number of seconds between ticks.

- In process(), check whether the tuple is a normal tuple or a tick tuple. When a tick tuple is received, the bolt should run its scheduled processing.

The intermediate rankings bolt

The intermediate rankings bolt maintains a dictionary of the top maxSize (10) items ranked by occurrence count, and emits those items every emitFrequencyInSeconds (15) seconds. In production, the topology will run many instances of this bolt, with each of them maintaining the top words for a *subset* of the overall words seen. Having many instances of the same component allows the topology to process large numbers of tweets and easily keep all the counts in the memory, even if the number of distinct words is quite large.

Enter this code in `intermediaterankings.py`:

```python
from petrel import storm
from petrel.emitter import BasicBolt

def tup_sort_key(tup):
    return tup.values[1]


class IntermediateRankingsBolt(BasicBolt):
    emitFrequencyInSeconds = 15
    maxSize = 10

    def __init__(self):
        super(IntermediateRankingsBolt,
            self).__init__(script=__file__)
        self.rankedItems = {}

    def declareOutputFields(self):
        return ['word', 'count']

    def process(self, tup):
        if tup.is_tick_tuple():
            for t in self.rankedItems.itervalues():
                storm.emit(t.values)
        else:
            self.rankedItems[tup.values[0]] = tup
            if len(self.rankedItems) > self.maxSize:
                for t in sorted(
                        self.rankedItems.itervalues(),
                        key=tup_sort_key):
                    del self.rankedItems[t.values[0]]
                    break

    def getComponentConfiguration(self):
        return {"topology.tick.tuple.freq.secs":
            self.emitFrequencyInSeconds}

def run():
    IntermediateRankingsBolt().run()
```

The total rankings bolt

The total rankings bolt is very similar to the intermediate rankings bolt. There is only one instance of this bolt in the topology. It receives the top words from each instance of that bolt, choosing the top `maxSize` (10) items overall.

Enter the following code in `totalrankings.py`:

```
import logging

from petrel import storm
from petrel.emitter import BasicBolt

log = logging.getLogger('totalrankings')

def tup_sort_key(tup):
    return tup.values[1]


class TotalRankingsBolt(BasicBolt):
    emitFrequencyInSeconds = 15
    maxSize = 10

    def __init__(self):
        super(TotalRankingsBolt, self).__init__(script=__file__)
        self.rankedItems = {}

    def declareOutputFields(self):
        return ['word', 'count']

    def process(self, tup):
        if tup.is_tick_tuple():
            for t in sorted(
                    self.rankedItems.itervalues(),
                    key=tup_sort_key,
                    reverse=True):
                log.info('Emitting: %s', repr(t.values))
                storm.emit(t.values)
        else:
            self.rankedItems[tup.values[0]] = tup
            if len(self.rankedItems) > self.maxSize:
                for t in sorted(
                        self.rankedItems.itervalues(),
                        key=tup_sort_key):
                    del self.rankedItems[t.values[0]]
```

```
                          break
            zero_keys = set(
                k for k, v in self.rankedItems.iteritems()
                if v.values[1] == 0)
            for k in zero_keys:
                del self.rankedItems[k]

    def getComponentConfiguration(self):
        return {"topology.tick.tuple.freq.secs":
            self.emitFrequencyInSeconds}

def run():
    TotalRankingsBolt().run()
```

Defining the topology

Here is the `create.py` script that defines the structure of the topology:

```python
from twitterstream import TwitterStreamSpout
from splitsentence import SplitSentenceBolt
from rollingcount import RollingCountBolt
from intermediaterankings import IntermediateRankingsBolt
from totalrankings import TotalRankingsBolt

def create(builder):
    spoutId = "spout"
    splitterId = "splitter"
    counterId = "counter"
    intermediateRankerId = "intermediateRanker"
    totalRankerId = "finalRanker"
    builder.setSpout(spoutId, TwitterStreamSpout(), 1)
    builder.setBolt(
        splitterId, SplitSentenceBolt(),
            1).shuffleGrouping("spout")
    builder.setBolt(
        counterId, RollingCountBolt(), 4).fieldsGrouping(
            splitterId, ["word"])
    builder.setBolt(
        intermediateRankerId,
        IntermediateRankingsBolt(), 4).fieldsGrouping(
            counterId, ["word"])
    builder.setBolt(
        totalRankerId, TotalRankingsBolt()).globalGrouping(
            intermediateRankerId)
```

The structure of this topology is similar to the word count topology from *Chapter 3, Introducing Petrel.* `TotalRankingsBolt` has a new wrinkle. As described earlier, there is just one instance of this bolt, and it uses `globalGrouping()`, so all tuples from `IntermediateRankingsBolt` are sent to it.

You may be wondering why the topology needs both an intermediate ranking and a total ranking bolt. In order for us to know the top words overall, there needs to be a single bolt instance (total rankings) that sees across the entire tweet stream. But at high data rates, a single bolt can't possibly keep up with the traffic. The intermediate rankings bolt instances "shield" the total rankings bolt from this traffic, computing the top words for their slice of the tweet stream. This allows the final rankings bolt to compute the most common words overall, while consuming only a handful of the overall word counts. Elegant!

Running the topology

We have a few more small items to address before we run the topology:

1. Copy the `logconfig.ini` file from the second example in *Chapter 3, Introducing Petrel*, to this topology's directory.

2. Create a file called `setup.sh`. Petrel will package this script with the topology and run it at startup. This script installs the third-party Python libraries used by the topology. The file looks like this:

   ```
   pip install -U pip
   pip install nltk==3.0.1 oauthlib==0.7.2 tweepy==3.2.0
   ```

3. Create a file called `manifest.txt` with these two lines:

   ```
   logconfig.ini
   setup.sh
   ```

4. Before running the topology, let's review the list of files that we've created. Make sure you have created these files correctly:

   - `topology.yaml`
   - `twitterstream.py`
   - `splitsentence.py`
   - `rollingcount.py`
   - `intermediaterankings.py`
   - `totalrankings.py`
   - `manifest.txt`
   - `setup.sh`

5. Run the topology with this command:

```
petrel submit --config topology.yaml --logdir `pwd`
```

Once the topology starts running, open another terminal in the `topology` directory. Enter the following command to see the `log` file for the total rankings bolt, sorted from oldest to newest:

```
ls -ltr petrel*totalrankings.log
```

If this is the first time you've run the topology, there will be only one log file listed. A new file is created for each run. If there are several files listed, choose the most recent one. Enter this command to monitor the contents of the log file (the exact filename will be different on your system):

```
tail -f petrel24748_totalrankings.log
```

About every 15 seconds, you will see log messages with the top 10 words in descending order of popularity, like this:

Summary

In this chapter, we developed a complex topology using a number of new techniques and libraries. After reading this example, you should be ready to begin applying Petrel and Storm to solve real problems.

In the upcoming chapter, we'll take a closer look at some of Storm's built-in features that are useful while operating a cluster, such as logging and monitoring.

5
Persistence Using Redis and MongoDB

It is often necessary to store tuples in a persistent data store, such as a NoSQL database or a fast key-value cache, in order to perform additional analysis. In this chapter, we will revisit the Twitter trending analysis topology from *Chapter 4, Example Topology – Twitter* with the help of two popular persistence media: Redis and MongoDB.

Redis (`http://redis.io/`) is an open source and BSD-licensed advanced key-value cache and store. MongoDB is a cross-platform, document-oriented database (`https://www.mongodb.org/`).

Here are the two problems that we will solve in this chapter:

- Finding the top trending tweet topics using Redis
- Computing hourly aggregates of city mentions using MongoDB

Finding the top n ranked topics using Redis

The topology will compute a rolling ranking of the most popular words in the past 5 minutes. The word counts are stored in individual windows of 60 seconds in length. It consists of the following components:

- Twitter stream spout (`twitterstream.py`): This reads tweets from the Twitter sample stream. This spout is unchanged from *Chapter 4, Example Topology – Twitter*.

- Splitter bolt (`splitsentence.py`): This receives tweets and splits them into words. This is also identical to the one in *Chapter 4, Example Topology – Twitter*.

- Rolling word count bolt (`rollingcount.py`): This receives words and counts the occurrences. The Redis keys look like `twitter_word_count:<start time of current window in seconds>`, and the values are stored in a hash using the following simple format:

```
{
    "word1": 5,
    "word2", 3,
}
```

This bolt uses the Redis `expireat` command to discard old data after 5 minutes. These lines of code perform the key work:

```
self.conn.zincrby(name, word)
self.conn.expireat(name, expires)
Total rankings bolt (totalrankings.py)
```

In this bolt, the following code does the most important work:

```
self.conn.zunionstore(
    'twitter_word_count',
    ['twitter_word_count:%s' % t for t in xrange(
        first_window, now_floor)])
for t in self.conn.zrevrange('twitter_word_count', 0, self.maxSize,
withscores=True):
    log.info('Emitting: %s', repr(t))
    storm.emit(t)
```

This bolt computes the top `maxSize` words across the last num_windows periods. The `zunionstore()` combines the word counts across the periods. The `zrevrange()` sorts the combined counts, returning the top `maxSize` words.

In the original Twitter example, roughly the same logic was implemented in `rollingcount.py`, `intermediaterankings.py`, and `totalrankings.py`. With Redis, we can implement the same calculations in just a few lines. The design delegates much of the work to Redis. Depending on your data volumes, this may not scale as well as the topology in the previous chapter. However, it demonstrates that Redis's capabilities go far beyond simply storing data.

The topology configuration file – the Redis case

Coming up is the topology configuration file. Depending on your Redis installation, you may need to change the value of `redis_url`.

Enter this code in `topology.yaml`:

```
nimbus.host: "localhost"
topology.workers: 1
oauth.consumer_key: "your-key-for-oauth-blah"
oauth.consumer_secret: "your-secret-for-oauth-blah"
oauth.access_token: "your-access-token-blah"
oauth.access_token_secret: "your-access-secret-blah"
twitter_word_count.redis_url: "redis://localhost:6379"
twitter_word_count.num_windows: 5
twitter_word_count.window_duration: 60
```

Rolling word count bolt – the Redis case

The rolling word count bolt is similar to the word count bolt in *Chapter 3,
Introducing Petrel*. The bolt in the earlier chapter simply accumulated the word count
indefinitely. This is not good for analyzing the top words on Twitter, where the
popular topics can change from one moment to the next. Rather, we want counts
that reflect the latest information. As explained earlier, the rolling word count
bolt stores data in time-based buckets. Then, it periodically discards buckets that
exceed 5 minutes in age. Thus, the word counts from this bolt only consider the
last 5 minutes of data.

Enter this code in `rollingcount.py`:

```
import math
import time
from collections import defaultdict

import redis

from petrel import storm
from petrel.emitter import BasicBolt

class RollingCountBolt(BasicBolt):
    def __init__(self):
        super(RollingCountBolt, self).__init__(script=__file__)
```

```
    def initialize(self, conf, context):
        self.conf = conf
        self.num_windows =
            self.conf['twitter_word_count.num_windows']
        self.window_duration =
            self.conf['twitter_word_count.window_duration']
        self.conn =
            redis.from_url(conf['twitter_word_count.redis_url'])

    @classmethod
    def declareOutputFields(cls):
        return ['word', 'count']

    def process(self, tup):
        word = tup.values[0]
        now = time.time()
        now_floor = int(math.floor(now / self.window_duration) *
            self.window_duration)
        expires = int(now_floor + self.num_windows *
            self.window_duration)
        name = 'twitter_word_count:%s' % now_floor
        self.conn.zincrby(name, word)
        self.conn.expireat(name, expires)

    def run():
        RollingCountBolt().run()
```

Total rankings bolt – the Redis case

Enter the following code in `totalrankings.py`:

```
import logging
import math
import time
import redis

from petrel import storm
from petrel.emitter import BasicBolt

log = logging.getLogger('totalrankings')

class TotalRankingsBolt(BasicBolt):
    emitFrequencyInSeconds = 15
    maxSize = 10
```

```
    def __init__(self):
        super(TotalRankingsBolt, self).__init__(script=__file__)
        self.rankedItems = {}

    def initialize(self, conf, context):
        self.conf = conf
          self.num_windows = \
            self.conf['twitter_word_count.num_windows']
        self.window_duration = \
            self.conf['twitter_word_count.window_duration']
        self.conn = redis.from_url(
            conf['twitter_word_count.redis_url'])

    def declareOutputFields(self):
        return ['word', 'count']

    def process(self, tup):
        if tup.is_tick_tuple():
            now = time.time()
            now_floor = int(math.floor(now / self.window_duration) *
                self.window_duration)
            first_window = int(now_floor - self.num_windows *
                self.window_duration)
            self.conn.zunionstore(
                'twitter_word_count',
                ['twitter_word_count:%s' % t for t in
xrange(first_window, now_floor)])
            for t in self.conn.zrevrange('
                'twitter_word_count', 0,
              self.maxSize, withScores=True):
                log.info('Emitting: %s', repr(t))
                storm.emit(t)
    def getComponentConfiguration(self):
            return {"topology.tick.tuple.freq.secs":
                self.emitFrequencyInSeconds}

def run():
    TotalRankingsBolt().run()
```

Defining the topology – the Redis case

Here is the `create.py` script that defines the structure of the topology:

```
from twitterstream import TwitterStreamSpout
from splitsentence import SplitSentenceBolt
from rollingcount import RollingCountBolt
from totalrankings import TotalRankingsBolt

def create(builder):
    spoutId = "spout"
    splitterId = "splitter"
    counterId = "counter"
    totalRankerId = "finalRanker"
    builder.setSpout(spoutId, TwitterStreamSpout(), 1)
    builder.setBolt(
        splitterId, SplitSentenceBolt(),
        1).shuffleGrouping("spout")
    builder.setBolt(
        counterId, RollingCountBolt(), 4).fieldsGrouping(
            splitterId, ["word"])
    builder.setBolt(
        totalRankerId, TotalRankingsBolt()).globalGrouping(
            counterId)
```

Running the topology – the Redis case

We have a few more small things to address before we run the topology:

1. Copy the `logconfig.ini` file from the second example in *Chapter 3, Introducing Petrel,* to this topology's directory.

2. Create a file called `setup.sh`. Petrel will package this script with the topology and run it at startup. This script installs the third-party Python libraries used by the topology. The file looks like this:
   ```
   pip install -U pip
   pip install nltk==3.0.1 oauthlib==0.7.2
   tweepy==3.2.0
   ```

3. Create a file called `manifest.txt` with these two lines:
   ```
   logconfig.ini
   setup.sh
   ```

4. Install the Redis server on a well-known node. All workers will store state here:

```
sudo apt-get install redis-server
```

5. Install the Python Redis client on all Storm worker machines:

```
sudo apt-get install python-redis
```

6. Before running the topology, let's review the list of files that we've created. Make sure you have created these files correctly:

   ° `topology.yaml`
   ° `twitterstream.py`
   ° `splitsentence.py`
   ° `rollingcount.py`
   ° `totalrankings.py`
   ° `manifest.txt`
   ° `setup.sh`

7. Run the topology with the following command:

```
petrel submit --config topology.yaml --logdir `pwd`
```

Once the topology is running, open another terminal in the topology directory. Enter this command to see the log file for the total rankings bolt, sorted from oldest to newest:

```
ls -ltr petrel*totalrankings.log
```

If this is the first time you are running the topology, there will be only one log file listed. A new file is created for each run. If there are several listed, choose the most recent one. Enter this command to monitor the contents of the log file (the exact filename will be different on your system):

```
tail -f petrel24748_totalrankings.log
```

Periodically, you will see an output like the following, listing the top 5 words in descending order of popularity:

Example output from `totalrankings`:

```
[2015-08-10 21:30:01,691] [totalrankings] [INFO] Emitting: ('love', 74.0)

[2015-08-10 21:30:01,691] [totalrankings] [INFO] Emitting: ('amp', 68.0)

[2015-08-10 21:30:01,691] [totalrankings] [INFO] Emitting: ('like', 67.0)

[2015-08-10 21:30:01,692] [totalrankings] [INFO] Emitting: ('zaynmalik',
61.0)
```

```
[2015-08-10 21:30:01,692] [totalrankings] [INFO] Emitting: ('mtvhottest',
61.0)
[2015-08-10 21:30:01,692] [totalrankings] [INFO] Emitting: ('get', 58.0)
[2015-08-10 21:30:01,692] [totalrankings] [INFO] Emitting: ('one', 49.0)
[2015-08-10 21:30:01,692] [totalrankings] [INFO] Emitting: ('follow', 46.0)
[2015-08-10 21:30:01,692] [totalrankings] [INFO] Emitting: ('u', 44.0)
[2015-08-10 21:30:01,692] [totalrankings] [INFO] Emitting: ('new', 38.0)
[2015-08-10 21:30:01,692] [totalrankings] [INFO] Emitting: ('much', 37.0)
```

Finding the hourly count of tweets by city name using MongoDB

MongoDB is a popular database for storing large amounts of data. It is designed for easy scalability across many nodes.

To run this topology, you first need to install MongoDB and configure some database-specific settings. This example uses a MongoDB database called `cities` with a collection named `minute`. In order to compute the counts by city and minute, we must create a unique index on the `cities.minute` collection. To do this, launch the MongoDB command-line client:

```
mongo
```

Create a unique index on the `cities.minute` collection:

```
use cities
db.minute.createIndex( { minute: 1, city: 1 }, { unique: true } )
```

This index stores a per minute time series of city counts in MongoDB. After running the example topology to capture some data, we'll run a standalone command-line script (`city_report.py`) to sum the per minute city counts by hour and city.

This is a variant of the earlier Twitter topology. This example uses the Python geotext library (`https://pypi.python.org/pypi/geotext`) to find city names in tweets.

Here is an overview of the topology:

- Read the tweets.
- Split them into words and find city names.
- In MongoDB, count the number of times a city is mentioned each minute.

- Twitter stream spout (`twitterstream.py`): This reads tweets from the Twitter sample stream.

- City count bolt (`citycount.py`): This finds city names and writes to MongoDB. It is similar to the `SplitSentenceBolt` from the Twitter sample, but after splitting by words, it looks for city names.

The `_get_words()` function here is slightly different from earlier examples. This is because geotext does not recognize lowercase strings as city names.

It creates or updates MongoDB records, taking advantage of the unique index on minute and city to accumulate the per minute counts.

This is a common pattern for representing time series data in MongoDB. Each record also includes an `hour` field. The `city_report.py` script uses this to compute the hourly counts.

Enter this code in `citycount.py`:

```
Import datetime
import logging
import geotext
import nltk.corpus
import pymongo

from petrel import storm
from petrel.emitter import BasicBolt

log = logging.getLogger('citycount')

class CityCountBolt(BasicBolt):
    def __init__(self):
        super(CityCountBolt, self).__init__(script=__file__)
        self.stop_words = set(nltk.corpus.stopwords.words('english'))
        self.stop_words.update(['http', 'https', 'rt'])
        self.stop_cities = set([
            'bay', 'best', 'deal', 'man', 'metro', 'of', 'un'])

    def initialize(self, conf, context):
        self.db = pymongo.MongoClient()

    def declareOutputFields(self):
        return []

    def process(self, tup):
        clean_text = ' '.join(w for w in
            self._get_words(tup.values[0]))
```

```
        places = geotext.GeoText(clean_text)
        now_minute = self._get_minute()
        now_hour = now_minute.replace(minute=0)
        for city in places.cities:
            city = city.lower()
            if city in self.stop_cities:
                continue
            log.info('Updating count: %s, %s, %s', now_hour,
            now_minute, city)
            self.db.cities.minute.update(
                {
                    'hour': now_hour,
                    'minute': now_minute,
                    'city': city
                },
                {'$inc': { 'count' : 1 } },
                upsert=True)

    @staticmethod
    def _get_minute():
        return datetime.datetime.now().replace(second=0,
        microsecond=0)

    def _get_words(self, sentence):
        for w in nltk.word_tokenize(sentence):
            wl = w.lower()
            if wl.isalpha() and wl not in self.stop_words:
                yield w


def run():
    CityCountBolt().run()
```

Defining the topology – the MongoDB case

Enter the following code in `create.py`:

```
from twitterstream import TwitterStreamSpout
from citycount import CityCountBolt

def create(builder):
    spoutId = "spout"
    cityCountId = "citycount"
    builder.setSpout(spoutId, TwitterStreamSpout(), 1)
    builder.setBolt(cityCountId, CityCountBolt(),
        1).shuffleGrouping("spout")
```

Running the topology – the MongoDB case

We have a few more small things to address before we run the topology:

1. Copy the `logconfig.ini` file from the second example in *Chapter 3, Introducing Petrel* to this topology's directory.

2. Create a file called `setup.sh`:

   ```
   pip install -U pip
   pip install nltk==3.0.1 oauthlib==0.7.2 tweepy==3.2.0
   geotext==0.1.0 pymongo==3.0.3
   ```

3. Next, create a file called `manifest.txt`. This is identical to the Redis example.

   Install the MongoDB server. On Ubuntu, you can use the instructions given at `http://docs.mongodb.org/manual/tutorial/install-mongodb-on-ubuntu/`.

4. Install the Python MongoDB client on all Storm worker machines:

   ```
   pip install pymongo==3.0.3
   ```

5. To verify that `pymongo` is installed and the index is created correctly, start an interactive Python session by running `python`. Then use this code:

   ```
   import pymongo
   from pymongo import MongoClient
   db = MongoClient()
   for index in db.cities.minute.list_indexes():
       print index
   ```

   You should see the following output. The second line is the index that we added:

   ```
   SON([(u'v', 1), (u'key', SON([(u'_id', 1)])), (u'name', u'_id_'),
   (u'ns', u'cities.minute')])
   ```

   ```
   SON([(u'v', 1), (u'unique', True), (u'key', SON([(u'minute',
   1.0), (u'city', 1.0)])), (u'name', u'minute_1_city_1'), (u'ns',
   u'cities.minute')])
   ```

6. Next, install `geotext`:

   ```
   pip install geotext==0.1.0
   ```

7. Before running the topology, let's review the list of files that we created. Make sure you have created these files correctly:

    ° `topology.yaml`

    ° `twitterstream.py`

    ° `citycount.py`

    ° `manifest.txt`

    ° `setup.sh`

8. Run the topology with the following command:

```
petrel submit --config topology.yaml --logdir `pwd`
```

The `city_report.py` file is a standalone script that generates a simple hourly report from the data inserted by the topology. This script uses MongoDB aggregation to compute the hourly totals. As noted earlier, the report depends on the presence of an `hour` field.

Enter this code in `city_report.py`:

```python
import pymongo

def main():
    db = pymongo.MongoClient()
    pipeline = [{
        '$group': {
            '_id':   { 'hour': '$hour', 'city': '$city' },
            'count': { '$sum': '$count' }
        }
    }]
    for r in db.cities.command('aggregate', 'minute',
        pipeline=pipeline)['result']:
        print '%s,%s,%s' % (r['_id']['city'], r['_id']['hour'],
            r['count'])

if __name__ == '__main__':
    main()
```

Summary

In this chapter, we saw how to use two popular NoSQL storage engines (Redis and MongoDB) with Storm. We also showed you how to create data in a topology and access it from other applications, demonstrating that Storm can be an effective part of an ETL pipeline.

6
Petrel in Practice

In previous chapters, we saw working examples of Storm topologies, both simple and complex. In doing so, however, we skipped some of the tools and techniques that you'll need while developing your own topologies:

- Storm is a great environment for running your code, but deploying to Storm (even on your local machine) adds complexity and takes extra time. We'll see how to test your spouts and bolts outside of Storm.

- When components run inside Storm, they can't read from the console, which prevents the use of pdb, the standard Python debugger. This chapter demonstrates Winpdb, an interactive debugging tool suitable for debugging components inside Storm.

- Storm lets you easily harness the power of many servers, but performance of your code still matters. In this chapter, we'll see some ways of measuring the performance of our topology's components.

Testing a bolt

Storm makes it easy to deploy and run Python topologies, but developing and testing them in Storm is challenging, whether running in standalone Storm or a full Storm deployment:

- Storm launches programs on your behalf—not only your Python code but auxiliary Java processes as well

- It controls the Python components' standard input and output channels

- The Python programs must respond regularly to heartbeat messages or be shut down by Storm

This makes it difficult to debug Storm topologies using the typical tools and techniques used for other pieces of Python code, such as the common technique of running from the command line and debugging with pdb.

Petrel's mock module helps us with this. It provides a simple, standalone Python container for testing simple topologies and verifying that the expected results are returned.

In Petrel terms, a **simple** topology is one that only outputs to the default stream and has no branches or loops. The `run_simple_topology()` assumes that the first component in the list is a spout, passing the output of each component to the next component in the sequence.

Example – testing SplitSentenceBolt

Let's look at an example. Here is the `splitsentence.py` file from the first example in *Chapter 3, Introducing Petrel* with a unit test added:

```
from nose.tools import assert_equal

from petrel import mock, storm
from petrel.emitter import BasicBolt

from randomsentence import RandomSentenceSpout

class SplitSentenceBolt(BasicBolt):
    def __init__(self):
        super(SplitSentenceBolt, self).__init__(script=__file__)

    def declareOutputFields(self):
        return ['word']

    def process(self, tup):
        words = tup.values[0].split(" ")
        for word in words:
          storm.emit([word])


def test():
    bolt = SplitSentenceBolt()
    mock_spout = mock.MockSpout(
        RandomSentenceSpout.declareOutputFields(),
        [["Madam, I'm Adam."]])
```

```
    result = mock.run_simple_topology(
        None, [mock_spout, bolt], result_type=mock.LIST)
        assert_equal([['Madam,'], ["I'm"], ['Adam.']], result[bolt])


def run():
    SplitSentenceBolt().run()
```

To run the test, enter the following commands:

pip install nosetests

1. First, install the Python nosetests library by running the following:

    pip install nosetests

2. Next, run this line:

    nosetests -v splitsentence.py

If all goes well, you'll see the following output:

splitsentence.test ... ok

```
----------------------------------------------------------------------
```

Ran 1 test in 0.001s

OK

Nose is a very powerful tool with many features. We won't cover it in detail here, but you can find the documentation at `https://nose.readthedocs.org/en/latest/`.

Example – testing SplitSentenceBolt with WordCountBolt

The next example shows how to test a sequence of related components. In the following code, we see a new version of `wordcount.py` that tests the interaction between `SplitSentenceBolt` and `WordCountBolt`:

```
from collections import defaultdict

from nose.tools import assert_equal

from petrel import mock, storm
from petrel.emitter import BasicBolt
```

```
from randomsentence import RandomSentenceSpout
from splitsentence import SplitSentenceBolt

class WordCountBolt(BasicBolt):
    def __init__(self):
        super(WordCountBolt, self).__init__(script=__file__)
        self._count = defaultdict(int)

    @classmethod
    def declareOutputFields(cls):
        return ['word', 'count']

    def process(self, tup):
        word = tup.values[0]
        self._count[word] += 1
        storm.emit([word, self._count[word]])


def test():
    ss_bolt = SplitSentenceBolt()
    wc_bolt = WordCountBolt()

    mock_spout = mock.MockSpout(
        RandomSentenceSpout.declareOutputFields(),
        [["the bart the"]])

     result = mock.run_simple_topology(
       None,
       [mock_spout, ss_bolt, wc_bolt],
       result_type=mock.LIST)
       assert_equal([['the', 1], ['bart', 1], ['the', 2]],
        result[wc_bolt])


def run():
    WordCountBolt().run()
```

The test is pretty straightforward; we simply instantiate both components and include them in the right sequence when calling mock.run_simple_topology().

Both example tests specify `result_type=mock.LIST` while calling `run_simple_topology()`. This parameter option tells Petrel which format to use when returning output tuples. The options include:

`STORM_TUPLE`

`LIST`

`TUPLE`

`NAMEDTUPLE`

Generally, `LIST` is a good choice for components with a small number of output fields, while `NAMEDTUPLE` is more readable for a larger number of fields (that is, by allowing the test to access result fields by field name rather than numeric indices). `STORM_TUPLE` is useful if the test needs to check other attributes of the result, for example, the lesser-used stream property.

Debugging

Until now, we've debugged topologies using log messages and automated tests. These techniques are very powerful, but sometimes it may be necessary to debug directly inside the Storm environment. For example, the problem may:

- Depend on running as a particular user
- Occur only with real data
- Occur only when there are many instances of the component running in parallel

This section introduces a tool for debugging inside Storm.

Winpdb is a portable, GUI-based debugger for Python, with support for embedded debugging. If you're not familiar with the term "embedded debugging", note this: it simply means that Winpdb can attach to a program that was launched in some other way and not necessarily from WinDbg or your command shell. For this reason, it is a good fit for debugging Petrel components that run in Storm.

Installing Winpdb

Activate your Petrel virtual environment and then use `pip` to install it:

```
source <virtualenv directory>/bin/activate
pip install winpdb
```

Add Winpdb breakpoint

In the `splitsentence.py` file, add the following at the beginning of the `run()` function:

```
import rpdb2
rpdb2.start_embedded_debugger('password')
```

The `'password'` value can be anything; this is simply the password that you will use in the next step to attach to `splitsentence.py`.

When this line of code executes, the script will freeze for a default period of 5 minutes, waiting for a debugger to attach.

Launching and attaching the debugger

Now run the topology:

```
petrel submit --config topology.yaml
```

Once you see log messages from the spout, you will know that the topology is up and running, so you can connect with the debugger.

Launch `Winpdb` simply by running `winpdb`.

For more details on how to use Winpdb for embedded debugging, see the documentation at `http://winpdb.org/docs/embedded-debugging/`.

When the window appears, select **File** | **Attach** from the menu. A password dialog will appear. Here, enter the same password that you passed to `start_embedded_debugger()` and click on the **OK** button, as shown in this screenshot:

Next, choose the process to attach to and click on **OK**, as shown in the following screenshot:

Now you'll see the main Winpdb window, with the line below the breakpoint highlighted. If you've used other debuggers, Winpdb should be straightforward to use. If you need help using Winpdb, the following tutorial is very good for you:

`https://code.google.com/p/winpdb/wiki/DebuggingTutorial.`

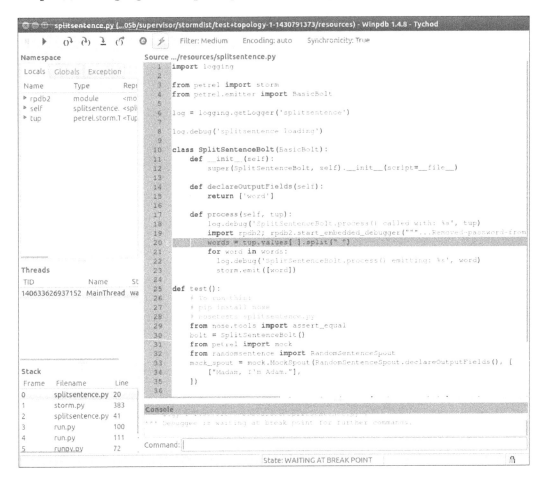

Profiling your topology's performance

Performance can be a concern for any application. This is true for Storm topologies as well, perhaps more so.

When you're trying to push a lot of data through a topology, raw performance is certainly a concern—faster components means that more data can be processed. But it's also important to understand the tuple processing performance of individual components. This information can be used in two ways.

The first is knowing which components are slower, because this tells you where to focus your attention if you are trying to make the code faster. Once you know which component (or components) is slow, you can use tools such as the Python cProfile module (`http://pymotw.com/2/profile/`) and the line profiler (`https://github.com/rkern/line_profiler`) to understand where the code is spending most of its time.

Even after profiling, some components will still be faster than others. In this case, understanding the relative performance between components can help you configure the topology for best performance.

This second point is somewhat subtle, so let's look at an example. In the following code, we see log excerpts for two Storm components from the word count topology. These log messages are generated automatically by Petrel. The first is the split sentence bolt, and the second is the word count bolt:

```
[2015-05-07 22:51:44,772] [storm] [DEBUG] BasicBolt profile:
total_num_tuples=79, num_tuples=79, avg_read_time=0.002431
(19.1%), avg_process_time=0.010279 (80.7%), avg_ack_time=0.000019
(0.2%)
[2015-05-07 22:51:45,776] [storm] [DEBUG] BasicBolt profile:
total_num_tuples=175, num_tuples=96, avg_read_time=0.000048
(0.5%), avg_process_time=0.010374 (99.3%), avg_ack_time=0.000025
(0.2%)
[2015-05-07 22:51:46,784] [storm] [DEBUG] BasicBolt profile:
total_num_tuples=271, num_tuples=96, avg_read_time=0.000043
(0.4%), avg_process_time=0.010417 (99.3%), avg_ack_time=0.000026
(0.2%)
[2015-05-07 22:51:47,791] [storm] [DEBUG] BasicBolt profile:
total_num_tuples=368, num_tuples=97, avg_read_time=0.000041
(0.4%), avg_process_time=0.010317 (99.4%), avg_ack_time=0.000021
(0.2%)
```

Split sentence bolt log

The following is the split sentence bolt log:

```
[2015-05-07 22:51:44,918] [storm] [DEBUG] BasicBolt profile:
total_num_tuples=591, num_tuples=591, avg_read_time=0.001623
(95.8%), avg_process_time=0.000052 (3.1%), avg_ack_time=0.000019
(1.1%)
[2015-05-07 22:51:45,924] [storm] [DEBUG] BasicBolt profile:
total_num_tuples=1215, num_tuples=624, avg_read_time=0.001523
(94.7%), avg_process_time=0.000060 (3.7%), avg_ack_time=0.000025
(1.5%)
```

```
[2015-05-07 22:51:46,930] [storm] [DEBUG] BasicBolt profile:
total_num_tuples=1829, num_tuples=614, avg_read_time=0.001559
(95.4%), avg_process_time=0.000055 (3.3%), avg_ack_time=0.000021
(1.3%)
[2015-05-07 22:51:47,938] [storm] [DEBUG] BasicBolt profile:
total_num_tuples=2451, num_tuples=622, avg_read_time=0.001547
(95.7%), avg_process_time=0.000049 (3.0%), avg_ack_time=0.000020
(1.3%)
```

Word count bolt log

These logs demonstrate that the split sentence bolt spends 0.010338 seconds processing and acknowledging each tuple (0.010317 + 0.000021), while the word count bolt spends 0.000069 seconds (0.000049 + 0.000020) per tuple. The split sentence bolt is slower, which suggests that you may want more instances of the split sentence bolt than the word count bolt.

> Why wasn't the read time considered in the preceding calculation? Read time includes the CPU time taken to read tuples from Storm, but it also includes time spent waiting (that is, sleeping) for the tuples to arrive. If the upstream component is providing data slowly, we don't want to count that time against our component. So for simplicity, we omitted the read time from the calculation.

Of course, the per-tuple performance is only part of the picture. You must also consider the sheer number of tuples to be processed. During the 4 seconds covered by the preceding logs, the split sentence bolt received 97 tuples (sentences), while the word count bolt received 622 tuples (words). Now we'll apply these numbers to the per-tuple processing times:

```
0.010338 seconds/tuple * 97 tuples = 1.002786 seconds (Split
sentence)
0.000069 seconds/tuple * 622 tuples = 0.042918 seconds (Word
count)
```

The total time used by the split sentence bolt is much larger (roughly 23 times greater), and we should take this into account while configuring the parallelism of the topology. For example, we might configure `topology.yaml` as follows:

```
petrel.parallelism.splitsentence: 24
petrel.parallelism.wordcount: 1
```

By configuring the topology in this way, we help ensure that at high traffic rates, there are enough split sentence bolts to avoid becoming a bottleneck, keeping the word count bolts busy all the time.

 The logs from the preceding section used a version of the split sentence bolt that was deliberately modified to run slower and make the example clearer.

Summary

In this chapter, you learned some skills that will help make you more productive building your own topologies. As you develop spouts or bolts, you can test them individually before assembling them into a complete topology and deploying on Storm. If you encounter a tricky problem that occurs only while running in Storm, you can use Winpdb in addition to (or instead of) log messages. When your code is working, you can get insights into which components take most of the time, so you can focus on improving performance in those areas. With these skills, you are now ready to go out and build your own topologies. Good luck!

Managing Storm Using Supervisord

This appendix gives you an overview of the following topics:

- Storm administration over a cluster
- Introducing supervisord
- Components of supervisord
- Supervisord installation and configuration

Storm administration over a cluster

There are many tools available that can create multiple virtual machines, install predefined software and even manage the state of that software.

Introducing supervisord

Supervisord is a process control system. It is a client-server system that allows its users to monitor and control a number of processes on Unix-like operating systems. For details, visit http://supervisord.org/.

Supervisord components

The server piece of the supervisor is known as supervisord. It is responsible for starting child programs upon its own invocation, responding to commands from clients, restarting crashed or exited subprocesses, logging its subprocess `stdout` and `stderr` output, and generating and handling "events" corresponding to points in subprocess lifetimes. The server process uses a configuration file. This is typically located in `/etc/supervisord.conf`. This configuration file is a Windows-INI style `config` file. It is important to keep this file secure via proper filesystem permissions because it might contain decrypted usernames and passwords:

- **supervisorctl**: The command-line client piece of the supervisor is known as supervisorctl. It provides a shell-like interface for the features provided by supervisord. From supervisorctl, a user can connect to different supervisord processes. They can get the status on the subprocesses controlled by, stop and start subprocesses of, and get lists of running processes of a supervisord. The command-line client talks to the server across a Unix domain socket or an Internet (TCP) socket. The server can assert that the user of a client should present authentication credentials before it allows them to use commands. The client process typically uses the same configuration file as the server, but any configuration file with a `[supervisorctl]` section in it will work.

- **Web server**: A (sparse) web user interface with functionality comparable to supervisorctl may be accessed via a browser if you start supervisord against an Internet socket. Visit the server URL (for example, `http://localhost:9001/`) to view and control the process status through the web interface after activating the configuration file's `[inet_http_server]` section.

- **XML-RPC interface**: The same HTTP server that serves the web UI serves up an XML-RPC interface that can be used to interrogate and control the supervisor and the programs it runs. See *XML-RPC API Documentation*.

- **Machines**: Let's assume that we have two EC2 machines of IP addresses `172-31-19-62` and `172.31.36.23`. We will install supervisord on both machines and later configure to decide what services of Storm would be running on each machine.

- **Storm and Zookeeper setup**: Let's run Zookeeper, Nimbus, supervisor, and the UI on machine `172.31.36.23` and only the supervisor on `172-31-19-62`.

- **Zookeeper version**: `zookeeper-3.4.6.tar.gz`.

- **Storm version**: `apache-storm-0.9.5.tar.gz`.

Here is the process of the Zookeeper server setup and configuration:

1. Download Zookeeper's latest version and extract it:

   ```
   tar -xvf zookeeper-3.4.6.tar.gz
   ```

2. Configure `zoo.cfg` in the `conf` directory to start Zookeeper in cluster mode.

3. Zookeeper conf:

   ```
   server.1=172.31.36.23:2888:3888
   tickTime=2000
   initLimit=10
   syncLimit=5
   # the directory where the snapshot is stored.
   dataDir=/home/ec2-user/zookeeper-3.4.6/tmp/zookeeper
   clientPort=2181
   ```

4. Make sure that the directory specified in `dataDir` is created and the user has read and write permissions on it.

5. Then, go to the Zookeeper `bin` directory and start the `zookeeper` server using the following command:

   ```
   [ec2-user@ip-172-31-36-23 bin~]$ zkServer.sh start
   ```

Storm server setup and configuration:

1. Download Storm's latest version from the Apache Storm website and extract it:

   ```
   tar -xvf apache-storm-0.9.5.tar.gz
   ```

2. Here is the configuration of the Storm Nimbus machine as well as the slave (added/changed configuration only):

   ```
   storm.zookeeper.servers: - "172.31.36.23"

   nimbus.host: "172.31.36.23"

   nimbus.childopts: "-Xmx1024m -Djava.net.preferIPv4Stack=true"

   ui.childopts: "-Xmx768m -Djava.net.preferIPv4Stack=true"

   supervisor.childopts: "-Djava.net.preferIPv4Stack=true"
   ```

```
worker.childopts: "-Xmx768m -Djava.net.preferIPv4Stack=true"

storm.local.dir: "/home/ec2-user/apache-storm-0.9.5/local"

supervisor.slots.ports:
    - 6700
    - 6701
    - 6702
    - 6703
```

Supervisord installation

It is possible to install supervisord by the following two ways:

1. Installing on a system with Internet access:

    Download the Setup tool and use the `easy_install` method.

2. Installing on a system without Internet access:

    Download all dependencies, copy to each machine, and then install it.

We will follow the second method of installation, the one in which Internet access is not required. We will download all dependencies and supervisord, and copy it to the servers.

Supervisord [`supervisor-3.1.3.tar.gz`] requires the following dependencies to be installed:

* Python 2.7 or later
* `setuptools` (latest) from `http://pypi.python.org/pypi/setuptools`
* `elementtree` (latest) from `http://effbot.org/downloads#elementtree.elementtree-1.2-20040618.tar.gz`
* `meld3-0.6.5.tar.gz`

Let's install supervisord and the necessary dependencies on both machines, `172.31.36.23` and `172-31-19-62`.

The following are the steps for installing the dependencies:

1. `setuptools`:
    - Unzip the `.zip` file using this command:

      `[ec2-user@ip-172-31-19-62 ~]$ tar -xvf setuptools-17.1.1.zip`

    - Go to the `setuptools-17.1.1` directory and run the installation command with `sudo`:

      `[ec2-user@ip-172-31-19-62 setuptools-17.1.1]$ sudo python setup.py install`

```
storm.zookeeper.servers: - "172.31.36.23"

nimbus.host: "172.31.36.23"

nimbus.childopts: "-Xmx1024m -Djava.net.preferIPv4Stack=true"

ui.childopts: "-Xmx768m -Djava.net.preferIPv4Stack=true"

supervisor.childopts: "-Djava.net.preferIPv4Stack=true"

worker.childopts: "-Xmx768m -Djava.net.preferIPv4Stack=true"

storm.local.dir: "/home/ec2-user/apache-storm-0.9.5/local"
```

```
supervisor.slots.ports:
  - 6700
  - 6701
  - 6702
  - 6703
```

2. `meld3`:

   ○ Extract the `.ts.gz` file using the following command:

   ```
   [ec2-user@ip-172-31-19-62 ~]$ tar -xvf meld3-0.6.5.tar.gz
   ```

   ○ Go to the `meld3.-0.6.5` directory and run this command:

   ```
   [ec2-user@ip-172-31-19-62 meld3-0.6.5]$ sudo pyth setup.py
   install
   ```

```
ec2-user@ip-172-31-19-62:~/meld3-0.6.5                                    _  □  X
[ec2-user@ip-172-31-19-62 meld3-0.6.5]$ ls
build          COPYRIGHT.txt  meld3      README.txt  TODO.txt
CHANGES.txt  LICENSE.txt    PKG-INFO   setup.py
[ec2-user@ip-172-31-19-62 meld3-0.6.5]$ sudo pyth setup.py install
```

3. `elementtree`:

   ○ Extract the `.ts.gz` file:

   ```
   [ec2-user@ip-172-31-19-62 ~]$ tar -xvf
   elementtree-1.2-20040618.tar.gz
   ```

   ○ Go to `elementtree-1.2-20040618` and run the following command:

   ```
   [ec2-user@ip-172-31-19-62 elementtree-1.2-20040618]$ sudo
   python setup.py install
   ```

```
ec2-user@ip-172-31-19-62:~/elementtree-1.2-20040618                    _  □  X

[ec2-user@ip-172-31-19-62 meld3-0.6.5]$ ls
build           COPYRIGHT.txt  meld3        README.txt  TODO.txt
CHANGES.txt  LICENSE.txt     PKG-INFO  setup.py
[ec2-user@ip-172-31-19-62 meld3-0.6.5]$ cd ..
[ec2-user@ip-172-31-19-62 ~]$ ls
apache-storm-0.9.5                 setuptools-17.1.1.zip
apache-storm-0.9.5.tar.gz          storm
elementtree-1.2-20040618           supervisor-3.1.3
elementtree-1.2-20040618.tar.gz    supervisor-3.1.3.tar.gz
epel-release-6-8.noarch.rpm        supervisord
h2db                               supervisord.conf
installable SupervisorD            supervisord.log
jdk-8u5-linux-x64.rpm              supervisord.pid
jzmq-2.1.0.el6.x86_64.rpm          supervisor.sock
meld3-0.6.5                        zeromq-2.1.7-1.el6.x86_64.rpm
meld3-0.6.5.tar.gz                 zookeeper-3.4.6
nohup.out                         zookeeper-3.4.6.tar.gz
setuptools-17.1.1                  zookeeper.out
[ec2-user@ip-172-31-19-62 ~]$ tar -xvf elementtree-1.2-20040618.tar.gz ^C
[ec2-user@ip-172-31-19-62 ~]$ cd elementtree-1.2-20040618
[ec2-user@ip-172-31-19-62 elementtree-1.2-20040618]$ sudo python setup.py install
1
```

The following are the supervisord installations:

- Extract supervisor-3.1.3 using this command:

  ```
  [ec2-user@ip-172-31-19-62 ~]$ tar -xvf supervisor-3.1.3.tar.gz
  ```

- Go to the supervisor-3.1.3 directory and run the following command:

  ```
  [ec2-user@ip-172-31-19-62 supervisor-3.1.3]$ sudo python setup.py
  install
  ```

```
[ec2-user@ip-172-31-19-62 ~]$ tar -xvf supervisor-3.1.3.tar.gz ^C
[ec2-user@ip-172-31-19-62 ~]$ cd supervisor-3.1.3
[ec2-user@ip-172-31-19-62 supervisor-3.1.3]$ ls
build           dist         PKG-INFO    supervisor        tox.ini
CHANGES.txt     docs         README.rst  supervisord.log
CONTRIBUTORS.txt  LICENSES.txt  setup.cfg   supervisor.egg-info
COPYRIGHT.txt   MANIFEST.in   setup.py    TODO.txt
[ec2-user@ip-172-31-19-62 supervisor-3.1.3]$ sudo python setup.py install ^C
[ec2-user@ip-172-31-19-62 supervisor-3.1.3]$
```

 A similar setup of supervisord is required on another machine, that is, 172.31.36.23.

Configuration of supervisord.conf

Lets configure services on the 172.31.36.23 machine and assume that the supervisord installation is done as explained previously. Once supervisor is installed, you can build the supervisord.conf file to start the supervisord and supervisorctl commands:

- Make the supervisor.conf file. Put it into the /etc directory.

- We can refer get sample supervisord.conf using the following command:

```
[ec2-user@ip-172-31-36-23 ~]$ echo_supervisord_conf
```

Take a look at the supervisord.conf file:

```
[unix_http_server]
file = /home/ec2-user/supervisor.sock
chmod = 0777

[inet_http_server]         ; inet (TCP) server disabled by default
port=172.31.36.23:9001        ; (ip_address:port specifier, *:port
for all iface)
username=user              ; (default is no username (open
server))
password=123               ; (default is no password (open
server))

[rpcinterface:supervisor]
supervisor.rpcinterface_factory =
supervisor.rpcinterface:make_main_rpcinterface

[supervisord]
logfile_backups=10              ; (num of main logfile rotation
backups;default 10)
logfile=/home/ec2-user/supervisord.log ; (main log file;default
$CWD/supervisord.log)
logfile_maxbytes=50MB           ; (max main logfile bytes b4
rotation;default 50MB)
pidfile=/home/ec2-user/supervisord.pid ; (supervisord
pidfile;default supervisord.pid)
nodaemon=false                  ; (start in foreground if
true;default false)
minfds=1024                     ; (min. avail startup file
descriptors;default 1024)

[supervisorctl]
;serverurl = unix:///home/ec2-user/supervisor.sock
serverurl=http://172.31.36.23:9001 ; use an http:// url to specify
an inet socket
```

```
;username=chris                  ; should be same as http_username if
set
;password=123                    ; should be same as http_password if
set
```

[program:storm-nimbus]
```
command=/home/ec2-user/apache-storm-0.9.5/bin/storm nimbus
user=ec2-user
autostart=false
autorestart=false
startsecs=10
startretries=999
log_stdout=true
log_stderr=true
stdout_logfile=/home/ec2-user/storm/logs/nimbus.out
logfile_maxbytes=20MB
logfile_backups=10
```

[program:storm-ui]
```
command=/home/ec2-user/apache-storm-0.9.5/bin/storm ui
user=ec2-user
autostart=false
autorestart=false
startsecs=10
startretries=999
log_stdout=true
log_stderr=true
stdout_logfile=/home/ec2-user/storm/logs/ui.out
logfile_maxbytes=20MB
logfile_backups=10
```

[program:storm-supervisor]
```
command=/home/ec2-user/apache-storm-0.9.5/bin/storm supervisor
user=ec2-user
autostart=false
autorestart=false
startsecs=10
startretries=999
log_stdout=true
log_stderr=true
stdout_logfile=/home/ec2-user/storm/logs/supervisor.out
logfile_maxbytes=20MB
logfile_backups=10
```

Start the supervisor server first:

```
[ec2-user@ip-172-31-36-23 ~] sudo /usr/bin/supervisord -c /etc/
supervisord.conf
```

Then, start all processes using `supervisorctl`:

```
[ec2-user@ip-172-31-36-23 ~] sudo /usr/bin/supervisorctl -c /etc/
supervisord.conf status
storm-nimbus                    STOPPED    Not started
storm-supervisor                STOPPED    Not started
storm-ui                        STOPPED    Not started
[ec2-user@ip-172-31-36-23 ~]$ sudo /usr/bin/supervisorctl -c /etc/
supervisord.conf start all
storm-supervisor: started
storm-ui: started
storm-nimbus: started
[ec2-user@ip-172-31-36-23 ~]$ jps
14452 Jps
13315 QuorumPeerMain
14255 nimbus
14233 supervisor
14234 core
[ec2-user@ip-172-31-36-23 ~]$
```

We can view the supervisord web UI and control processes on the browser. `52.11.193.108` is the public IP address of the `172-31-36-23` machine (`http://52.11.193.108:9001`):

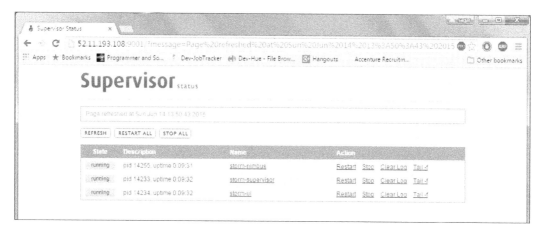

Configuration of supervisord.conf on 172-31-19-62

Keep only the following services in the configuration file:

```
[unix_http_server]
[rpcinterface:supervisor]
[supervisord]
[supervisorctl]
[program:storm-supervisor]
```

After that, you can start the supervisor server and all processes using `supervisorctl` on `172-31-19-62` machine.

Summary

In this chapter, we saw how distributed Storm processes running over multiple machines can be managed using the supervisord process. There are many options available in supervisord, such as `autostart=true`. If we set this option for any Storm process, it also increases the reliability of the overall system and manages failure of Nimbus.

Index

Symbol

_get_words() function 71

B

bolt
  SplitSentenceBolt, testing 76, 77
  SplitSentenceBolt, testing with
    WordCountBolt 77-79
  testing 75, 76

C

cluster modes, Storm
  about 4
  developer mode 4
  multimachine 5
  single-machine 4
  Storm client 5, 6

D

Data Specification Language (DSL) 3
debugging 79
declareOutputFields() function 34
distributed computation
  scaling 28
Distributed Remote Procedure
    Call (DRPC) 10

E

easy_install method 90
elementtree
  URL 90

executer 17, 18

Extraction, Transformation, and
    Load (ETL) 2

G

Git
  URL 7

I

installation, Storm
  about 6
  native (Netty only) dependency 8
  optional configurations, using 11
  Zookeeper 6, 7

J

jps command 6

K

key features, Storm 3

M

MongoDB
  topology, defining 72
  topology, running 73, 74
  URL 63
  used, for finding hourly count of tweets by
    city 70, 71

Y

yaml configuration
URL 11

Z

Zookeeper
about 4, 14
installation 7
installation, URL 6
setup, URL 7

Thank you for buying
Building Python Real-Time Applications with Storm

About Packt Publishing

Packt, pronounced 'packed', published its first book, *Mastering phpMyAdmin for Effective MySQL Management*, in April 2004, and subsequently continued to specialize in publishing highly focused books on specific technologies and solutions.

Our books and publications share the experiences of your fellow IT professionals in adapting and customizing today's systems, applications, and frameworks. Our solution-based books give you the knowledge and power to customize the software and technologies you're using to get the job done. Packt books are more specific and less general than the IT books you have seen in the past. Our unique business model allows us to bring you more focused information, giving you more of what you need to know, and less of what you don't.

Packt is a modern yet unique publishing company that focuses on producing quality, cutting-edge books for communities of developers, administrators, and newbies alike. For more information, please visit our website at www.packtpub.com.

About Packt Open Source

In 2010, Packt launched two new brands, Packt Open Source and Packt Enterprise, in order to continue its focus on specialization. This book is part of the Packt Open Source brand, home to books published on software built around open source licenses, and offering information to anybody from advanced developers to budding web designers. The Open Source brand also runs Packt's Open Source Royalty Scheme, by which Packt gives a royalty to each open source project about whose software a book is sold.

Writing for Packt

We welcome all inquiries from people who are interested in authoring. Book proposals should be sent to author@packtpub.com. If your book idea is still at an early stage and you would like to discuss it first before writing a formal book proposal, then please contact us; one of our commissioning editors will get in touch with you.

We're not just looking for published authors; if you have strong technical skills but no writing experience, our experienced editors can help you develop a writing career, or simply get some additional reward for your expertise.

Expert Python Programming

ISBN: 978-1-84719-494-7   Paperback: 372 pages

Best practices for designing, coding, and distributing your Python software

1. Learn Python development best practices from an expert, with detailed coverage of naming and coding conventions.

2. Apply object-oriented principles, design patterns, and advanced syntax tricks.

3. Manage your code with distributed version control.

4. Profile and optimize your code.

5. Proactive test-driven development and continuous integration.

Learning Storm

ISBN: 978-1-78398-132-8   Paperback: 252 pages

Create real-time stream processing applications with Apache Storm

1. Integrate Storm with other Big Data technologies like Hadoop, HBase, and Apache Kafka.

2. Explore log processing and machine learning using Storm.

3. Step-by-step and easy-to-understand guide to effortlessly create applications with Storm.

Please check **www.PacktPub.com** for information on our titles

Storm Blueprints: Patterns for Distributed Real-time Computation

ISBN: 978-1-78216-829-4   Paperback: 336 pages

Use Storm design patterns to perform distributed, real-time big data processing, and analytics for real-world use cases

1. Process high-volume log files in real time while learning the fundamentals of Storm topologies and system deployment.

2. Deploy Storm on Hadoop (YARN) and understand how the systems complement each other for online advertising and trade processing.

3. Follow along as each chapter presents a new problem and the architectural pattern, design, and implementation of a solution.

Storm Real-time Processing Cookbook

ISBN: 978-1-78216-442-5   Paperback: 254 pages

Efficiently process unbounded streams of data in real time

1. Learn the key concepts of processing data in real time with Storm.

2. Concepts ranging from Log stream processing to mastering data management with Storm.

3. Written in a Cookbook style, with plenty of practical recipes with well-explained code examples and relevant screenshots and diagrams.

Please check **www.PacktPub.com** for information on our titles

www.ingramcontent.com/pod-product-compliance
Lightning Source LLC
Chambersburg PA
CBHW060155060326
40690CB00018B/4125